Crime and Everyday Life

THE PINE FORGE PRESS SOCIAL SCIENCE LIBRARY

The McDonaldization of Society: An Investigation Into the Changing Character of Contemporary Social Life *by George Ritzer*

Sociological Snapshots: Seeing Social Structure and Change in Everyday Life *by Jack Levin*

What Is Society? Reflections on Freedom, Order, and Change *by Earl Babbie*

The Production of Reality: Essays and Readings in Social Psychology *by Peter Kollock and Jodi O'Brien*

Adventures in Social Research: Data Analysis Using SPSS® *by Earl Babbie and Fred Halley*

Crime and Everyday Life: Insights and Implications for Society *by Marcus Felson*

Sociology of Work: Perspectives, Analyses, Issues *by Richard H. Hall*

Aging: Concepts and Controversies *by Harry R. Moody, Jr.*

Worlds of Difference: Inequality in the Aging Experience *by Eleanor Palo Stoller and Rose Campbell Gibson*

Forthcoming

Sociology for a New Century *A Pine Forge Press Series edited by Charles Ragin, Wendy Griswold, and Larry Griffin*

- **Social Psychology and Social Institutions** *by Denise D. and William T. Bielby*
- **The Social Ecology of Natural Resources and Development** *by Stephen G. Bunker*
- **How Societies Change** *by Daniel Chirot*
- **Ethnic Dynamics in the Modern World: Continuity and Transformation** *by Stephen Cornell*
- **Sociology of Childhood** *by William A. Corsaro*
- **Cultures and Societies in a Changing World** *by Wendy Griswold*
- **Crime and Disrepute: Comparative Perspectives** *by John Hagan*
- **Racism and the Modern World: Sociological Perspectives** *by Wilmot James*
- **Religion in the Global Village** *by Lester Kurtz*
- **Waves of Democracy** *by John Markoff*
- **Organizations in a World Economy** *by Walter W. Powell*
- **Constructing Social Research** *by Charles C. Ragin*
- **Women, Men, and Work** *by Barbara Reskin and Irene Padavic*
- **Cities in a World Economy** *by Saskia Sassen*

Crime and Everyday Life

Insights and Implications for Society

Marcus Felson

University of Southern California

PINE FORGE PRESS

Thousand Oaks • London • New Delhi

For information, address:

 Pine Forge Press
A Sage Publications Company
2455 Teller Road
Thousand Oaks, California 91320

Copy Editor: Steven Summerlight
Production Editor: Judith L. Hunter
Designer: Lisa S. Mirski
Typesetter: Christina M. Hill
Cover: Paula Shuhert
Printer: Malloy Lithographing, Inc.

Printed in the United States of America
2 3 4 5 6 7 8 9 10—97 96 95 95 94

Library of Congress Cataloging-in-Publication Data

Felson, Marcus.
    Crime and everyday life : insights and implications for society /
Marcus Felson.
        p.   cm. — (The Pine Forge Press social science library)
    Includes bibliographical references and index.
    ISBN 0-8039-9029-4 (alk. paper : pbk.)
    1. Crime—United States. 2. Crime prevention—United States.
3. Social control—United States. I. Title. II. Series.
HV6789.F45   1994
364.973—dc20   93-8566
                                                                    CIP

I dedicate this book to my parents, who marched to their own drummers while remaining a team for more than half a century. My father, the late Ben Felson, made his unique contributions to radiology by gathering information as directly as possible from nature itself. My mother, Virginia Raphaelson Felson, always an independent woman, was one of the few of her era to graduate from college. In her seventh decade of life, she has gone back to the university again because she likes reading thick books, going to long lectures, and arguing with her professors on interesting substantive matters. To the extent that I have a critical mind, it comes from them.

About the Author

Marcus Felson (Ph.D., University of Michigan) is a criminologist at the University of Southern California, where he serves as both Professor of Sociology and Senior Research Associate at the Social Science Research Institute. He has written more than 60 research articles. *Routine Activity and Rational Choice,* coedited with Ronald V. Clarke, has just been published as Volume 5 of *Advances in Criminological Theory.*

About the Publisher

Pine Forge Press is a new educational publisher, dedicated to publishing innovative books and software throughout the social sciences. On this and any other of our publications, we welcome your comments, ideas, and suggestions. Please call or write to

Pine Forge Press
A Sage Publications Company
2455 Teller Road
Thousand Oaks, CA 91320
805-499-4224
Internet: sdr@pfp.sagepub.com

Contents

Preface

This is a book about how the United States developed and maintains its huge crime rates.[1] These high crime rates persisted under Democrats and Republicans alike and put to shame the anticrime policies of conventional liberals and conservatives. The criminal justice system increasingly spends billions of dollars and yet leaves us with little more than a sense of futility. U.S. society has obviously failed to grapple with and solve its festering crime problem. Nor can we claim that criminology as a field knew all along what to do, if only people had listened.

Just at the time when U.S. society has most needed to broaden its intellectual perspective on crime, just the opposite happened. The level of political discussion on crime has deteriorated to an embarrassing level, while the news and entertainment media coverage of crime has filled peoples' minds not only with a variety of specific misconceptions but also with a basically inaccurate image of crime and criminals. Their coverage has an implicit bias: The more interesting and unusual crimes make better TV shows and news stories, while the more routine and representative crimes are neglected. As a result, the misinformed public can only err in thinking about crime and what to do about it.

This book seeks to help the reader gain critical freedom from these biases and to think more creatively about how crime occurs and what to do to prevent it. This means reducing our intellectual and practical expectations of the criminal justice system, which does not even receive reports on most of the offenses that occur and cannot do much about most of those that are reported. Any society that has to rely on these slow and uncertain public agencies as the main sources of prevention has already lost the battle against crime.

This volume presents the *routine activity approach* to crime analysis and crime prevention. We focus on crime incidents rather than on offenders themselves, examining how these incidents originate in the routine activities of everyday life. One of the most important features of such activities is their contribution to informal social control, a quiet and natural method by which people prevent crime in the course of daily life. This control occurs as people interact and bring out the best in one another. When informal control is working, society minimizes its reliance on police and prisons for preventing crime, putting these backup agencies into sporadic action when all else has failed.

Informal control offers simple, benign, unobtrusive, and inexpensive contributions to crime prevention such as:

- the peacemaker who keeps an argument between two people from escalating into something far worse;

- the neighbors who look after one anothers' property;

- the office receptionist who asks, "May I help you?" to those who wander in, discouraging crime without threatening anybody;

- the family that spends time together, naturally avoiding crime situations;

- the business person who quietly designs crime control into his or her everyday business practices.

None of these examples emphasizes violence or the criminal justice system, and yet each is extremely effective in preventing crime. In these examples, informal social control occurs in specific settings as a matter of course, so gently that you hardly know it is there. Such "natural" crime prevention acts early rather than letting trouble escalate, reducing temptation rather than inviting people to commit crime and trying to apprehend them afterward.

To develop ideas for natural crime prevention, this book draws from a broader perspective of several disciplines. Thus in using biology we discuss nutrition and its impact on physical development (Chapter 5) rather than talk about the more conventional topic of the genetic inheritance of criminality. We gather ideas from situational and environmental psychology (Chapters 2 and 7) rather than studying personalities of criminals. Looking back in time, we rely on human ecology for a sketch of changes in everyday life (Chapters 3 and 4) and a modern description of traditional work tasks (Chapter 5). In our exploration of crime and control in the future (Chapter 9), we consider the impact of communications and computer technologies in human terms. We suggest that developing technologies have a surprise for U.S. society: a chance to strengthen local communities, increase controls, and thus reduce crime.

This book takes a strong stand against our society's conventional liberal and conservative positions about crime, neither of which are practical for crime prevention and both of which ignore much of what is known about crime. They are driven by their own agendas and do not wish to be confused with facts about crime as a private phenomenon largely impervious to state intervention. Both approaches distract us from the important topic of informal social control and the recognition that crime is very human behavior indeed. Students of crime must be encouraged to think originally and to go beyond canned ideologies and failed policies. A new criminology is needed for the future. By taking a risk with new ideas, we can help make a brighter future for our students and our field of study.

Endnote

---

1. Between 1963 and 1975, the FBI's Uniform Crime Reports showed tripling and quadrupling of major crime rates in the United States, which were not that low in the first place. This pattern of dramatic increase holds for the best-reported crime categories—homicide and auto theft—assuring us that these are real trends, not merely increased reporting. These increases occurred controlling for the size of the population, and only a small part of the change could be attributed to the entry of the baby boom into high-crime ages. When the baby boom began to pass out of those ages after 1975, if crime rates should have fallen dramatically, they did not do so. The Uniform Crime Reports indicate that crime rates went up even further during some of these years, while during the 1980s the National Crime Survey (based on a survey of the general public rather than official data) showed crime rates to have stabilized at very high levels. For more on these sources, see Chapter 1, p. 2, and footnote 4, p. 23.

Acknowledgments

This book would not have been written without Ronald V. Clarke, who suggested that I write it and encouraged me to stick with it. Travis Hirschi stoically read through several iterations; I should have listened to his advice in the first place. I am also grateful for comments from Hugh Barlow, Paul and Pat Brantingham, John Dombrink, Richard Felson, Steve Shilo Felson, Daniel Glaser, Sol Kobrin, Jan Gorecki, Michael Gottfredson, Carl-Gunnar Janson, David A. Karp, Edward Kawakami, Brendan Kremer, Scott McNall, Lourdes Ongkeko, and Niko Pfund. Remaining errors are at least 97% mine.

Ideas from many authors are incorporated into this volume, including my many students, who taught me at least as much as I taught them. The Social Science Research Institute at the University of Southern California graciously provided me a home for almost a decade. There I received frequent assistance and nurturing from true professionals: Letty Baz, Elaine Corry, Ward Edwards, Eli Heitz, Cheryl Maxson, Judith Webb, and Malcolm Klein, the last of whom also read a tortuous early version of this manuscript.

The School of Criminal Justice at Rutgers University in Newark, New Jersey, and the University of Stockholm, Sweden, provided me with places to visit for more than half a year each. My previous employer, the University of Illinois at Urbana-Champaign, gave shelter for a dozen years, and its wonderful library made all the difference in the world.

This volume was finalized while I was Principal Investigator for the Crime-Free Environments Project, funded by the National Institute of Justice (Grant 91-IJ-CX-KO21). What I learned on that project has influenced me in many ways. For that I wish to share credit with Scott Santoro, Project Coordinator; Richard Titus, NIJ's Project Monitor; our dozen able staff members; and hundreds of anonymous respondents.

I appreciate deeply my teachers from Walnut Hills High School in Cincinnati, the University of Chicago, and the University of Michigan. I only hope I can show my students their level of dedication.

1

Fallacies and Truths About Crime

Education consists mainly
in what we have unlearned.

—*Mark Twain Notebook (1935)*

Many people begin studying crime with a mind full of distracting emotions and misconceptions.[1] The emotions might include extreme sympathy for or antipathy against offenders, victims, police officers, or the criminal justice system. Perhaps because of these emotions, many people make sweeping generalizations about crime, such as the following:

- "We ought to lock up all the criminals and throw away the key."
- "Most rape victims bring it on themselves."
- "Racism is the cause of most of our crime."
- "Americans are taught to be violent."

Perhaps such statements deserve discussion, but the strong emotions underlying them often interfere with that discussion and make it hard to sift out that grain of truth. The purpose of this chapter is to try to take a more objective view.

Emotions are not the only problem in studying crime. Because crime is so widely discussed, incorrect information about crime is widely believed. The reader has to reexamine some "common knowledge." Fortunately, most people also have some correct information about crime. This chapter is devoted to not only helping overcome misinformation, but also reinforcing correct information about crime.

This volume builds a general perspective that helps to organize crime information: "the routine activity approach."[2] This perspective treats crime as a routine activity that draws on other routine activities. Chapter 2 outlines the approach, but this chapter prepares our foundations by explaining the common elements of crime incidents as they occur in the

---

Citations may be found in the endnotes section at the back of each chapter.

tangible world. The chapter plan is first to present fallacies about crime and then to present truths, before summarizing what we have covered.

Our first step is to try to free ourselves from mass media images of crime.[3]

Sources Showing Crime
as Ordinary

Crimes are generally dramatic and serious in police adventure shows on television and when reported as news. Violent incidents predominate. This leads to the *dramatic fallacy* of crime analysis, because crime is portrayed as much more dramatic than it usually is. For example, watching television at night or reading the newspaper in the morning, one is likely to see a great deal of murder, especially romantic murders by jealous lovers, as well as felons and police officers shooting at one another.

To understand the dramatic fallacy, it is important to learn more about crime in its ordinary forms. The following three standard sources of crime data can help us.[4]

1. *Official police reports.* Each local police department collects crime data and reports it routinely to the Federal Bureau of Investigation in Washington, D.C. The FBI compiles these statistics for the United States as a whole and publishes them annually in its *Uniform Crime Reports* (all data refer to the year preceding the report date).

2. *Victim surveys.* Data on crime are collected through such efforts as the National Crime Survey, which interviews a general sample of citizens about their own and their households' victimization experiences. This survey is conducted by the U.S. Bureau of the Census and turns up at least twice as many crimes (in the categories asked) as official police data.

3. *Self-reports.* Based on interviews with youths or others about their own lawbreaking, these surveys report many more crimes than do official police data. They are especially effective in turning up reports of underage crimes (status offenses), minor drug abuse, and minor thefts.

All three types of crime data lead to the conclusion that most crime is very ordinary.

Official Data

To establish this point, we begin with data from the FBI's *Uniform Crime Reports* for 1990. These include a total of 14.5 million offenses reported for eight major crime categories alone: homicide,[5] forcible rape, aggravated assault, robbery, burglary, motor vehicle theft, larceny-theft, and arson.[6] Yet almost 9 out of 10 of these crimes are property crimes: burglaries, motor vehicle thefts, and larceny-thefts. Homicides are only two-tenths of 1% of the major crime total—and we have not yet begun to consider all the minor offenses.

Most of the 20,045 homicides in the United States in 1990 would not interest Sherlock Holmes: Only 312 were by strangulation, 36 by drowning, 14 by explosives, and 11 by poison. Only 65 of these homicides were killings of law enforcement officers: only one-third of 1% of all homicides in the United States that year. Only 2% of 1990 homicides involved romantic triangles, and only 6.5% involved narcotics felons. And not all of these offenses are very interesting. This is not to deny the significance of these deaths, but it does point out that interesting homicides are such a small share of total homicides and an even tinier share of major crimes.

Now if we turn to the 9 million arrests in 1990 for all reasons, four out of five were not even for the eight major crimes. For example, more than 1 million were for driving under the influence of alcohol, and another 1.5 million arrests were for drunkenness, disorderly conduct, and liquor law violations. In other words, for every homicide in the United States, there are some 500 arrests of all types and many more crimes that never lead to arrest.

Victim Reports

The National Crime Survey indicated approximately 34 million victimizations in the United States in 1990.[7] Some 81% of the victimizations reported were nonviolent. If we compare the 20,045 homicides officially reported to the 4.7 million assaults from the National Crime Survey, we see that for every homicide there are at least 230 nonlethal assaults mentioned by respondents.

Self-Reports

Again, survey responses are dominated by relatively minor crimes. For example, 88% of high school students reported illegal alcohol use; another 31% reported having used marijuana.[8] Yet less than 7% reported ever having used cocaine, for which current use is reported by 2% of respondents. Again, minor offenses greatly outnumber major ones.

Thus the vast majority of crimes are very ordinary, undramatic, and certainly nonviolent. Examples of common criminal acts are shoplifting, public drunkenness, disturbing the peace, breaking and entering, smoking small amounts of marijuana, stealing car accessories or contents, vandalizing park property, and stealing company property from the workplace. Even when there is violence, it usually is minor and leaves no lasting physical harm. Indeed, an incident in which two drunk fellows ineptly shove one another is much more typical than a gunfight.

These common offenses are not the stuff of television. So-called cop shows prefer dramatic plots, interesting offenses, stunning fights, and thrilling car chases—anything but ordinary criminal acts. Even homicide is treated not in its ordinary form: the tragic result of a stupid little quarrel.[9] The television medium is more likely to present a clever and dramatic murder with a plot that fills a half-hour or hour time slot and a level of drama and excitement that are absent from the ordinary real life murder or mugging.

Police officers will tell you that their work involves hours and hours of boredom that are interrupted by moments of sheer terror. Yet most police officers never fire their weapons on the job and only a tiny fraction have ever shot or much less killed anybody. For example, compared to almost 3,900 homicides in California in 1991, there were only 131 cases of police officers killing suspects in what were judged to be "justifiable" homicides.[10] That means there were 30 ordinary homicides for every police killing.

In recent years, several television networks have discovered that they can film and present live police activities.[11] These shows give a better portrayal of the daily life of police officers and offenders than had previous cop shows. However, even these shows have a natural bias toward action. One would never guess from them that police spend a lot of time driving around waiting for something to happen. The more ordinary encounters with citizens are not likely to be included. Thus the new cop shows compress what action there is into a kaleidoscope of excitement and quick diversity. Even these rather realistic shows miss one important point about real crime: The majority of crime is either never reported to the police or results in no police action when it is reported. Thus even the most realistic cop show is still a kind of fiction. If the producers tried to show the boredom of everyday police work, their programs would have no viewers.

Newspapers offer more space than does television for covering ordinary criminal events, but only college, community, or small-town newspapers take the trouble to write about an ordinary break-in or theft of a car stereo. Major newspapers in big cities will not cover these incidents. Even commonplace murders (such as those resulting from ordinary arguments) are usually given short shrift in big city newspapers or are left out entirely; it is the unusual gang slaying and the drive-by shooting that is featured.[12] Such coverage leads many people to believe that they know a lot more about crime than they really do.

The Brilliant and Daring Criminal?

Closely related to the dramatic fallacy is the *ingenuity fallacy*. This is the tendency to exaggerate the offender's cleverness. In the adventures of Sherlock Holmes, Professor Moriarty is an example of an evil and brilliant daredevil, whom Sherlock Holmes can only catch after an epic struggle.[13]

Another example of the skilled criminal is the cat burglar, who can slip into a room while his victims sleep, quietly pocket their valuables, and then slip out.[14] Yet most residential burglaries are conducted mainly in daytime when homes are deserted, not at night when greater skill would be required. Those that do occur at night generally occur when people are out for the evening or away on vacation. Paul Cromwell and his associates (1991) carried out an elaborate and clever ethnographic study of known burglars. The researchers drove around with their subjects to stage imaginary burglaries, asking such questions as:

- Would you break into that house?
- Why would you not you break into that other house?
- What attracts you to the house on the corner?
- Why would you not break in right now?

Almost all of the burglars said that they would never enter a residence that they knew to be occupied! This is why they probe to make sure nobody is home. The most common method for probing is to knock on the door or ring the doorbell. But first these burglars drive around awhile to pick their targets. They take a look, think quickly, home in on the target, and then act. Although many of their decisions are intuitive, they have an underlying rationale: They pick times and places that offer good targets but have little chance of getting caught.

On numerous occasions, crime victims have stated, "It must have been a professional who broke into our house." Yet after they recite the facts of the case, it becomes clear that almost anybody could have committed the crime. Almost anybody knows to look for jewels hidden in the bathroom or kitchen. Almost any teenage offender can get into the house in less than a minute and out in another minute or two with some loot. Almost anybody can succeed at burglary in a neighborhood largely abandoned during the daytime.

The "de-skilling" of crime in recent history is an important insight of Maurice Cusson of the University of Montreal.[15] During the era of the convergent city, household density was so high that only a skilled burglar could sneak in and out successfully. Before the self-service store existed, only a skilled thief could slip the merchandise out from under a shopkeeper's nose. The changes in household activity patterns (see Chapter 4) and marketing patterns (see Chapter 5) provided great new crime opportunities that required little or no skill. Even bank robberies today are mostly unplanned, with the offender typically robbing the bank after seeing it for the first time.[16]

The ingenuity fallacy also leads many people to overestimate the amount of centrally organized crime in society, the role of gangs, the role of organized crime, and the role of conspiracy. Even though many crimes are committed by groups, this does not mean that such groups are well organized, carefully coordinated, or widely linked.

Malcolm Klein, an expert on juvenile gangs, reports that such gangs are typically loose networks with unstable membership. Few are well organized or persistent, and those that do persist have subgangs that come and go. In addition, most of the crime committed in gang territories are not organized by gangs. This misconception has led much of the public to see gangs as the central crime problem rather than putting them into the larger perspective of a generally high crime rate.[17]

The same issue is relevant for organized crime. The news media and many movies depict "the Mafia" as a centrally organized group functioning much as a business board. Although this may be true in Sicily and southern Italy, the American version of organized crime is much less centralized and more a network of people who act illegally but do not work from the same location. Some but not all of these criminals know one another, sharing illegal acts but not acting as a board of directors. This point is made most effectively by Peter Reuter (1984). A senior economist at the Rand Corporation, Reuter has examined illegal markets and attempts by organized crime to control them. These markets include bookmaking, "numbers" rackets, and loan sharking. These markets are not controlled in a centralized fashion as they are with a television Mafia.[18]

How Old Are Criminals?

A third fallacy is the *age fallacy*, which leads people to think that both offenders and victims of crime are older than criminologists know them to be.[19] Television often presents offenders and victims of crime who are middle-aged or older. Yet victim surveys repeatedly show that ordinary crime victimization risk is highest among teenagers and those in their early 20s. This risk declines noticeably in the late 20s, and the decline continues into the later ages. Except for purse snatching, the relative victimization risk is very low for senior citizens, however much their suffering may interest the mass media.

Offending also shows a young pattern. When victims of violence in the National Crime Survey were asked to estimate the ages of their attackers, 61% of victims younger than 21 reported that the offenders were 21 or younger. For victims 21 to 29 years of age, only one in four report the offenders to be older than their own age group. In general, the tendency to participate in crime shoots up with the onset of adolescence, peaks in the mid to later teens, and declines from there on. After age 30, the decline in crime participation is especially marked.

The age pattern of crime can be offset by changes in the opportunity to carry out crime. For example, those too young to have a job do not get a chance to engage in employee theft, so these crimes will not begin until they enter the labor force (see end of Chapter 5). The lack of opportunity may also explain why 54% of those arrested for murder are older than 25, even though other assaults have a younger pattern. Think of murder as a special case of assault in which the victim usually dies because the offender uses a more lethal weapon. Survey data indicate that aging brings higher levels of gun ownership, hence a greater chance for an assault to become a murder.[20]

Criminal justice system data tend to overestimate the age of offenders, because so many are transferred quickly to the juvenile system and treated leniently. Even so, four fifths of arrested burglars are younger than 30 and two thirds are younger than 25.

To sum up, we have reviewed fallacies about both crime and criminals. Both are quite ordinary. Offenders tend to be adolescents or young adults. Although they may act in groups, seldom are they sophisticated in their organization. We now turn to the role of the criminal justice system.

Are the Police and Courts Central to Crime?

The *constabulary fallacy* is the unfortunate tendency to think that the police know about crimes that have been committed and are the key to crime prevention. To be sure, crime is very important for police, but how important are police for crime? The same general question can be asked about judges, prosecutors, and corrections personnel.

Reporting Crime

Respondents to the National Crime Survey report that 63% of their victimizations were never reported to police. For thefts and household larceny victimizations, this figure exceeded 70%. Self-report data turn up even greater numbers of illegal acts never gaining the attention of police, notably in the area of smoking marijuana and underage use of alcohol.[21] When so much crime never comes to the attention of police, we have to begin putting police power and the criminal justice system as a whole into a smaller perspective.

The Short Arm of the Law

Of those crimes that police know to exist, the vast majority result in no arrest; of those arrested, most do not lead to trial or a guilty plea; of those that get to trial, most do not result in incarceration. For example, some 5.1 million household burglaries were estimated nationally from the 1990 National Crime Survey. Table 1.1 shows what happens with every 1,000 of these burglaries: More than 600 are never reported to the police, 960 do not result in arrest, 987 do not lead to conviction for burglary, and some 990 are never sentenced to jail or prison. Of those who are sentenced, not all are actually locked up, because of jail and prison overcrowding.

Table 1.1 Dispositions of Household Burglaries

Household burglaries	1,000
Burglaries reported*	390
Burglary arrests	40
Burglary convictions (state courts)	13
Incarceration	10

*Uniform Crime Reports

Derived from 1991 *Sourcebook*, Tables 3.1, 3.2, 3.127, 4.1, 4.2, 5.46, 5.47, and 5.49. The table does not present true rates, because of time lags and differences in definition. These calculations should be treated as estimates only.

The fallout from start to finish is even greater for some other crimes. For example, the National Crime Survey estimates 21 million larcenies nationally in 1990, but only 61,918 people were sentenced to incarceration for larceny (3 per 1,000). These data suggest that the criminal justice system is actually quite marginal in its direct effect on everyday crime.

Delays in Punishment

Even when the criminal justice system delivers punishment, it does so after long delays. For example, the median time elapsing between arrest for larceny and conviction in state courts in 1988 was five months, with a mean of eight months! These delays occur despite the fact that 93% of larceny convictions involve a guilty plea and do not even require trial.[22] And most trials are bench trials (before a judge and without a jury).[23]

To put our system of punishment into perspective, consider what happens when you touch a hot stove: You receive quick, certain, but minor pain. After being burned once, you will not touch a hot stove again. Now think of an imaginary hot stove that burns you only once every 500 times you touch it, with the burn not hurting until five months later. Psychological research and common sense alike tell us this imaginary stove will not be as effective in punishing us as the real stove. Such a pattern of rewards and punishments is called a *reinforcement schedule*.[24] Psychologists have established the following:

*   rewards work better than punishments,
*   reinforcements work better when they quickly follow the event,
*   reinforcements work better when they are frequent, and
*   extreme reinforcements are not very effective.

We can see that the U.S. criminal justice system does everything wrong: It gives punishments rather than rewards and relies on rare and delayed— but extreme—penalties. Meanwhile, crime gives sure and quick rewards to offenders. It should come as no surprise that so many people continue to commit crimes.

Patrol and Protect?

Even without punishment, police theoretically can reduce crime by patrolling and thus, by their sheer presence on the streets, reduce crime. The Kansas City Patrol Experiment investigated this point by making major increases in police patrols and then testing the impact of such increases. The experiment discovered that intensified police patrols are scarcely noticed by offenders or citizens and have no impact on crime rates.[25]

The problem is not that police on patrol do something wrong, but rather that we are giving them a ridiculously impossible task and should not be surprised when they do not gain success. We are asking them to protect one quarter of 1 billion people and billions of pieces of property dispersed over vast amounts of space. The modern metropolis as we know it is so spread out that it defeats effective policing (see Chapter 4).

To illustrate how difficult it is to cover a police beat for all 168 hours in a week, let us do some calculations. Note that at least one third of sworn police officers have special assignments or full-time desk duties and cannot patrol at all. Consider also that each patrol officer works approximately 10 hours per week on roll call, paperwork, court appearances, instruction, consultation, and breaks, leaving 30 hours per week for actual patrol. Assume that each officer patrols alone.

Consider Los Angeles County as an example. Its 8.8 million people live in 4,070 square miles at a density of 2,178 persons per square mile or approximately 1,000 households per square mile. Los Angeles County has some 15,000 police officers who must cover (by the above arithmetic) approximately 1,670 beats of some 2.4 square miles each. That means that each officer on patrol has to "protect" approximately 2,400 households and several hundred businesses, schools, and other locations every day. Round it off to some 3,000 locations that must be protected by each officer on patrol. Each location can expect daily coverage of approximately 29 seconds.[26]

That is not only precious little direct protection, but also little time for an officer to learn who has a right to be walking out of your place and who does not. It is not surprising that less than 1% of offenses end with the offender "caught in the act" by police on patrol. Doubling the number of police in a U.S. metropolis is like doubling a drop in a bucket.

Does Bad Come From Bad?

We now turn to misconceptions about how crime relates to other phenomena in society.

This section examines the *pestilence fallacy*, which states that bad things come from other bad things. Crime is bad. Therefore it must emerge from other ills, such as unemployment, poverty, cruelty, and the like. Moreover, prosperity ought to bring lower crime rates.

Why then do the most prosperous nations of the world, including the United States, have high property crime rates? Why do the poor nations of the world have generally low property crime rates? Why does the United States, despite its prosperity, have such high violent crime rates? Why does the Netherlands, despite its high level of social welfare spending and emphasis on social equality, also have high violent crime rates? Why was the major period of crime rate increase in the United States, 1963 to 1975, also a period of healthy economic growth and relatively low unemployment?[27]

Why did Sweden's crime rates increase greatly as its Social Democratic government brought more and more programs to enhance equality and protect the poor? For example, Sweden had some 8,000 violent crimes in 1950, which increased to nearly 40,000 in 1988.[28] During the same period, burglaries grew to 7 times their former number, and robberies increased to 20 times their former level! This is not to argue that Sweden's welfare state contributed to its crime rate (nonwelfare states also had proliferating crime), but to show that crime seems to march to its own drummer, largely ignoring social justice, inequality, government social policy, welfare systems, poverty, unemployment, and the like. To the extent that crime rates respond at all to these phenomena, they may actually rise somewhat with prosperity. In any case, crime does not simply flow from other ills. This is not an argument against fighting poverty, discrimination, or unemployment. Rather, it is an attempt to detach criminology from a knee-jerk link to other social problems.

These points show that we still have a puzzle to piece together.

Liberals, Conservatives, or Neither?

All too many observers tend to link crime to their larger political or religious agenda. This might be called the *agenda fallacy*. For example, a "liberal" agenda promises to reduce crime by enacting poverty programs and increasing social or economic justice. A "conservative" agenda offers to reduce crime by decreasing welfare support or by using capital punishment (even though it does not apply to most crimes).[29] Some religious groups claim that conversion to their faith or values will prevent crime. In each case, crime is treated not for its own sake but rather for how it can be added to a larger agenda.

If you are in favor of a minimum wage as part of your agenda, then why not argue that it will prevent crime? If you are in favor of more emphasis on sexual morality, tell people this will lead to crime prevention. If you are a feminist, proclaim that rape is produced by antifeminism. If you dislike pornography, link it to sexual or other crimes. If the entertainment media offend your sensibilities, blame them for crime and demand censorship as a crime prevention method. Right-wing, left-wing, or whatever your agenda, if there is something you oppose, blame that for crime; if there is something you favor, link that to crime prevention! These are political tactics, but they are not the tactics for gaining more knowledge.

Indeed, they may eventually do harm to the agenda when promises are not fulfilled.

Those who really want to learn about crime should observe the following advice:

1. Learn everything you can about crime—for its own sake rather than to satisfy ulterior motives, such as gaining political power or religious converts.

2. Set your agenda aside while learning about crime. If your political and religious ideas are worthwhile, they should stand on their own merits.

Morality Among Mortals

A special case of the pestilence fallacy is the *morality fallacy*. This is the belief that crime is produced by declining morality. The fallacy follows from this line of thinking:

> Crime is immoral.
>
> Crime is widespread.
>
> Thus moral training is lacking.

The above reasoning forgets about hypocrisy. People are quite able to believe in and even to preach in favor of the very rules that they violate.

Moral *training* does not guarantee moral *behavior*, any more than the lack of moral behavior proves the absence of moral training. More specifically, the high murder rate in the United States does not prove that Americans believe in murder or that they are trained to commit murder. If that were the case, why do U.S. laws set such high levels of punishment for murder? Why would U.S. public opinion show such outrage at murderers and other serious criminals?

Consider a parallel question: Why do people become overweight? This set of statements is analogous to the earlier triplet of crime statements:

> Being overweight is bad.
>
> Being overweight is widespread.
>
> Thus thinness training is lacking.

If this conclusion is true, then why do so many overweight people want to lose weight? They must already know that it is better to be thin but find it difficult to accomplish their goal. Temptations to eat are widespread.

The problem for eating is the same as for drinking, drugs, and crime: to resist temptations.

The many fallacies reviewed so far fit a pattern. All of them point toward a general image of crime and criminals based on a moral struggle between evil offenders and the criminal justice system, which acts on behalf of society. Although we would like to think that the image is only present in the popular media, it is also found within criminology itself.[30]

Criminology Is Vulnerable

As Table 1.2 indicates, theories of criminality found in standard criminology textbooks are sometimes influenced by the same fallacies, if not in their original theoretical formulations, then at least as the theories are actually used by the policy world.[31]

Table 1.2 Fallacies in Criminality Theories

Theory	Policy Emphasis	Fallacies
Deterrence	Impact of punishment for deterring offenders; use capital punishment	A C D M
Incapacitation	Locking up "career" offenders	A C G I M
Differential association	"Bad company" creates delinquency; break up delinquency groups	A C P
Labeling	The criminal justice system labels people as deviant, thus reinforcing their criminal behavior	A C M P
Strain	Poverty and inequality produce crime	A M P

Fallacy types

A:	agenda fallacy	I:	ingenuity fallacy
C:	constabulary fallacy	M:	morality fallacy
D:	dramatic fallacy	P:	pestilence fallacy
G:	age fallacy		

Deterrence theory emphasizes using the criminal justice system to punish offenders. Ignoring the low probability of punishment in the United States (the constabulary fallacy), the theory's interest in capital punishment commits the dramatic fallacy, because most ordinary crimes are not even subject to capital punishment and ordinary murders are not likely to lead to capital sentences. Deterrence theory has become part of a self-righteousness political agenda from the right wing (agenda and morality fallacies).

Incapacitation theory advocates locking up "career" criminals to reduce crime. It exaggerates the criminal efficiency of a few people (the ingenuity fallacy) and forgets that these people will be locked up relatively late in their "criminal careers," after most of their damage has already been done (age fallacy). It relies too much on a criminal justice system (constabulary fallacy), is part of a right-wing political agenda, and depends too heavily on condemnation of a few (agenda and morality fallacies).

Differential association theory is based on the notion that delinquency is passed through associations. Thus delinquents are thought to "breed" other delinquents (pestilence fallacy). When the theory leads to a policy of having police try to break up delinquency groupings, the constabulary fallacy comes to play. When the theory is used to justify urban renewal of poor neighborhoods to "break the cycle of crime," the agenda fallacy is operating. Despite this critique of differential association theory, we shall draw a useful idea from it later in this chapter.

Labeling theory blames the criminal justice system for producing crime and delinquency as it "labels" individuals as deviant. Like deterrence and incapacitation theory, labeling theory greatly overestimates the power of the criminal justice system (constabulary fallacy). It treats crime as one ill arising from another, the evil of state power (hence the pestilence fallacy). The theory treats punishment in immoral terms and is part of a left-wing agenda.

Strain theory examines the strains in society as the cause of crime. Its central argument is that poor people seek the goals of society but cannot meet them by legitimate means; they then turn to illegitimate means. Crime prevention must therefore rely on reducing poverty. Strain theory commits the pestilence fallacy by linking crime to poverty. A moral tone underlies its approach, and it is part of a liberal agenda.

Control theory avoids most of the fallacies of the other theories. Rather than asking "Why does that bad boy commit crime?" control theory asks, "Why doesn't everyone commit crime?" The answer is that social controls influence people to follow society's rules. Thus control theory avoids reliance on the police, considers undramatic crimes, and minimizes moralistic analysis of crime and agenda fallacies. Control theory is taken up later in this chapter.

So far we have found some pieces of the crime puzzle: the ordinary nature of crime and criminals, the youthfulness of offenders and victims, the limited powers of police and the justice system, that crime can come from social goods as well as from ills, and that agendas and morality are not very helpful in approaching crime. Many other insights and facts about crime can help us to continue building our understanding of how crime occurs and how crime rates change. The next part of the chapter gathers some of these "truths."

Common Insights About Crime

This section presents six related common insights about human beings. These insights will help us examine how human situations vary and how they contribute to our understanding of crime. Some of the most useful insights about the human race in general can be applied to understand criminal behavior in particular.

First, consider the insight of *basic human frailty*. This is nothing more than the biblical notion that human beings are morally weak and that each individual needs help from society in order to withstand immoral temptations and pressures. Thus people with moral beliefs have difficulty meeting their own standards in practice, being capable of good and evil. The practical problem is to help people overcome their weaknesses by structuring society to reduce temptation. To be sure, some people are more "frail" than others, but all people have some frailty and temptability. This is quite different from saying people do not have strong enough beliefs about right and wrong. Rather it states that people have difficulty putting their moral beliefs into action, that is, in resisting temptations.

Second, related to the frailty insight, individuals vary greatly in their behavior from one situation to another. This *situational insight* is that each individual varies, not only over a lifetime but also in different situations on any given day. Almost everyone has ups and downs, ins and outs, anger and calm, conformity and defiance, and legal and illegal behavior. This insight has been incorporated into a whole social science field known as *situational social psychology*. Although they do not deny that individuals have personalities, situational social psychologists believe that the stability of personality is often exaggerated, that specific situations also have powerful effects on individuals.

Are youths as likely to get drunk with their parents present or absent? Are they as likely to smoke marijuana with peers as with their grandparents? Are those who are well behaved at home equally well behaved at school? Is sexual intercourse no more likely to occur when a couple is alone than when they are encumbered by the presence of others? Is juvenile delinquency no more likely to occur among a group of juveniles than it is when one juvenile is alone? Do the same students who are quiet in a college class remain quiet at a college football game? Are employees as likely to follow company rules when the boss is absent as when he or she is present? Do people drink as much alone as in a group? Are males no more rowdy among other males than they are in the presence of females?

If you answer "no" to several of these questions, then you accept the basic notion that much of human behavior is situational. That means that such behavior depends in part on who is present, where, and when.

The situational insight also helps us to think about the human frailty insight. Some situations will tend to bring out human weaknesses, including a weakness for crime.

Third, a special case of the situational insight is the *temptation insight*. In some situations, individuals are exposed to tremendous temptations. For example, self-service stores often place valuable and popular consumer goods within easy reach. This temptation helps to produce criminal acts that almost surely would not otherwise occur. One saying, "Opportunity makes the thief," reflects this insight. Flashing money among strangers, putting valuables in highly visible places, leaving keys in the car—all are examples of how to tempt someone to commit a crime that might not otherwise occur. Under some circumstances, one can be drawn to violate one's own beliefs.

Fourth, another special case of the situational insight is the *provocation insight*, which recognizes that an otherwise calm person can be provoked into a nasty, even violent, response. As discussed in Chapter 2, provocation is sometimes carried out by a third party who acts as a troublemaker by egging on two others until they have little choice but to fight or lose face. As we shall see, young males are more likely to create provocative situations, thus encouraging fights to happen.

Fifth, the *bad company insight* is the widespread recognition that going around with the "wrong crowd" is somehow associated with criminal behavior and delinquency. This insight was taken up in the previous section, which discussed differential association theory. This theory states that associating with other delinquents teaches an individual to become a delinquent and thus is a cause of delinquency. However, this theory has a problem: Like the chicken and the egg, it is difficult to measure which came first, bad company or one's own bad behavior. The expression "Birds of a feather fly together" may help explain why delinquents spend time together. In other words, an individual who seeks trouble may find a delinquent group to join him; but it is not clear that the others are any more or less at fault. Each parent may think "My child is a good child; it's those others who are a bad influence." This interpretation may make a parent feel better, but it does not tell us where delinquency starts.

Can each parent be correct? *Is it possible for all the boys to have a bad influence on one another?* Rather than being one-sided, bad influence is symmetrical; boys get into trouble together they would not get into separately. This "symmetrically bad influence" combines readily with the idea that human behavior is highly situational and that individuals are morally frail and subject to temptations and provocations. It is indeed possible for each boy to be a "good boy" at home but a "bad boy" when he runs with his peers. The issue is not so much bad company as adolescent company. *Each* boy is influenced by the group to do "bad" things. *Each* parent underestimates the situational variations and each child's potential for mischief.

Moreover, for technical reasons alone, groups can be better for carrying out some delinquent acts. It is easier to break into a house when there is a big boy to kick in the door, a fast boy as a lookout to run in with a warning, a dexterous boy to pick locks, and a large enough group to provide safety in numbers and mutual reinforcement of courage to break the law.

Sixth, consider the *idleness insight*. The expression "Idle hands are the devil's workshop" is central to control theory. Youths with nothing to do have a tendency to get into more trouble, while youths with a tight and busy schedule are more likely to stay out of trouble. Keeping busy might be accomplished by spending time at school, in family settings, in recreation, or at work. However, the idleness insight is not always so easy to apply in practice. Chapter 5 discusses the troubling finding that jobs for teenagers today do not reduce their involvement in delinquency. In Chapter 6, we show that schools may actually contribute to more crime by assembling teenagers with supervision that is too diluted over space. Chapter 7 discusses a program for gangs that actually served to perpetuate gang activity. The crime prevention discussion in Chapter 8 argues that programs for today's youths must take into account the fact that both parents are working and are likely to arrive home late. So the idleness insight poses a special challenge for analysis in today's society.

These six insights about human behavior are consistent with one another. They tell us that human beings are morally frail, temptable, provocative, responsive to situations and to one another, and influenced by idleness or activity. These six different points of departure all converge on the same image of human beings and the same image of the criminal as a human being.

Understanding our common humanity is important for studying how we as human beings can go wrong. But we also need to understand human variations.

The Individual Still Exists

Traditionally, criminology has focused on variations among individuals and neglected variations among situations. This book does not propose to turn the tables all the way. Some features of individuals remain important to criminology and need to be understood. Unfortunately, it is very difficult to explain why some individuals tend more to commit crime than others. Even though criminology has not yet "solved" this problem, more active offenders do have some traits that distinguish them from the rest of the population. In particular, we would find that the most active criminal offenders have a strong tendency to get into all kinds of trouble, criminal or not. Very active offenders are more likely, for example, to be crime victims, smokers, alcohol abusers, and bad drivers and to have trouble in school, work, and family relationships.[32]

In addition, frequent offenders have strong tendencies to commit a great variety of offenses rather than to specialize, say, in robbery or in burglary. Robbers usually have committed burglary or theft or have been caught speeding or charged with disorderly conduct. A look at criminal records of offenders displays this great variety of illegal experience, as does self-reported delinquency. Although some frequent offenders tend not to perform violent crimes, the violent offender's crime record usually includes more nonviolent crimes than violent crimes.

In general, we can say that some individuals have more trouble than others in resisting temptations of various kinds. The attraction of *self-*

control is that it sums up the efforts of parents, teachers, and others to counteract human frailty. We are all born weak, but year after year we are taught self-control to help us resist the various temptations; to keep us studying or working, out of the kitchen, or away from the bottle; to help keep the mouth shut when the boss, customer, spouse, or teacher says something that tempts a nasty reply; to avoid fights, drugs, and thefts; and to keep doing one's homework or one's work.

The self-control insight recognizes that some people often have a general tendency to get into trouble, especially by going for the pleasure of the moment. Other people have a general tendency to stay out of trouble and to perform those tasks that require delayed gratification—that is, giving up some pleasure now in order to improve things later. However, all people are subject to some temptation some of the time.

Importance of the Family

The *family insight* is the widely held notion that strong families impair crime and that weak families contribute to more crime.[33] Robert Sampson argues that family life—rather than poverty itself—is the driving force of crime production. The correlation between poverty and family problems is important, but it can also mislead us into thinking that poverty itself is the cause of crime when family problems contribute most directly to crime. By making clear when poverty is and is not associated with weak families, one can resolve the poverty fallacy and fit some more pieces of the "puzzle" together.

The family insight fits well with the other common insights.[34] Favorable families tend to combat basic human frailty, keep youths away from unfavorable situations, lead them away from bad company, idleness, undesirable temptations, risks, and provocations, while developing self-control when it is needed. Moreover, control theory tells us that children are often afraid to embarrass their parents by getting into trouble. Family life also serves to reduce crime victimization risk, as Chapter 2 explains.

Summary Thus Far

In sum, crime and delinquency are ordinary and undramatic, involve little ingenuity, draw offenders and victims who are much younger than is commonly believed, and are far less tied to the police and criminal justice system than is commonly stated. Crime derives from many of the good aspects of society, independent of popular agendas that wish to subsume it, is neither determined by poverty nor totally unrelated to it, and does not depend on morality as commonly portrayed.

Crime and delinquency feed on human frailty; depend on widespread situational variations in human behavior; are fed by temptations, provocations, exposure to bad company and idleness; and are countered by the development of self-control to resist temptation and strong family life. Even though these developments may contribute to a pattern of criminal behavior for certain individuals, that should not distract us from studying crime as a set of specific acts tempting a broad range of population.

It Is Not Who You Are,
but What You Did

A cornerstone of the U.S. legal system is that a person cannot be charged with a crime based on *who* he or she is, only for *what* he or she has done. Thus the state cannot charge a citizen with the crime of "being a drug abuser" or "a burglar." The state could charge him or her with "breaking into the residence at 341 Bryant Street on May 5, 1993." Specifics are required in search warrants and arrest warrants, as well as in the prosecution of the case. Only after someone is convicted of a specific crime and is ready for sentencing can the court make use of a previous criminal record.[35]

A lawyer's job is to take each case one at a time. A criminologist, in contrast, studies many cases to learn generalizations about crime. This often tempts criminologists to describe a world of criminals distinct from the world of general citizens.[36] We must resist that temptation. In the words of British scholar Susan Smith (1986, p. 98), "Empirical research is increasingly gnawing away at the concept of mutually exclusive offender and victim populations, showing it to be a figment of political imagination and a sop to social conscience." In an excellent collection of evidence on this point, Ezzat Fattah (1991) explains that both offenders and victims tend to be in the same groups: young, male, and unmarried. Offenders themselves have very high rates of crime victimization. In addition, the very high rates of self-reported delinquency among American youths and the arrest of adults without significant previous criminal records also tell us to abandon the notion that crime is the province of a small segment of the population.[37]

In the old cowboy movies, the roles were clearly divided into good guys (white hats and white horses) and bad guys (black hats and black horses). Criminology should not follow such a simpleminded script; what we know about crime does not justify that. Even though a few people commit a disproportionate share of crimes, millions of Americans commit a very few crimes each, which adds to millions of crimes in the aggregate.

This chapter has provided a general perspective, an image of crime and criminals. That image could be summed up in two words: *temptation* and *control*. Society provides temptations to commit crime as well as controls to prevent people from following these temptations. Some temptations are implicit in the human race and all human society, other temptations are generated by all modern societies, and still others are unique to our society. As any society generates more temptations but fewer controls, it invites a crime wave.

The task of the rest of this book is to study the structure of temptation and control. Society offers such a structure by organizing everyday life: work, school, shopping, streets, and transport. This daily organization influences crime by determining which of the two forces, temptation or control, has the upper hand in any given setting or in society as a whole.

This chapter has offered us a general image of crime and criminals. The next chapter will sharpen that image.

Questions for Writing, Reflection, and Debate

1. The author presents several fallacies and insights concerning crime and criminals. On each list, one item is general enough to include several other items. For each list, name that item and then discuss it.

2. Does this author's argument imply a *complete* change in the relationship between criminology and morality? Is this a proposal for a new criminology that is entirely amoral?

3. What does this chapter imply about the role of police and the rest of the criminal justice system?

4. The last paragraph of the chapter uses two summary words: *temptation* and *control*. Take all the insights about crime presented earlier and relate them to these two categories.

Sources for Ideas

Many of the ideas in this chapter derive from Hirschi (1969), who suggests that we should not ask "Why did the criminal do it?" but rather "Why does *everyone* not commit crime and delinquency?" Hirschi's answer is that people are tied into society and hence discouraged from committing crime. Their commitments to the future, their attachments to one another, and their involvements in conventional activities keep them from putting criminal thoughts into action.

Another source of ideas about crime is Gottfredson and Hirschi's *A General Theory of Crime* (1990). This controversial but fascinating book really should not be controversial at all. It emphasizes many of the fundamentals of crime, including the significance of male youths, and the general problem of self-control. In reading this book, try not to get lost in the various controversies among professional criminologists. Instead, pay attention to the image of the criminal presented by the authors.

The approach of this volume is also influenced by Maurice Cusson's *Why Delinquency?* (1983). This is a good translation of a very articulate book originally written in French. It presents the "strategic analysis" of crime, which takes into account how offenders think about what they do. Rather than taking offenders as irrational and immoral, Cusson analyzes offenders as human beings not much different from other human beings in many respects.

Endnotes

1. See Walker (1989) for a discussion of the emotional and sensational treatment of crime.

2. See Cohen and Felson (1979) and Felson (1987a). See also the landmark work on life-styles and crime: Hindelang, Gottfredson, and Garafolo (1978). Important related work on similar theories is reviewed in the introduction to Clarke and Felson (1993).

3. On myth making of crime by media and others, see Kappeler, Blumberg, and Potter (1993).

4. The four main statistical sources of information on crime used for this text are (a) *official police data*, which are collected in the FBI's annual *Uniform Crime Reports* (all data refer to the year preceding the report date); (b) *victimization data*, which are from the National Crime Survey and are found in the U.S.

Department of Justice's *Criminal Victimization in the United States*, various years (data from this large survey are used to estimate numbers for the entire nation); (c) *self-report data* from various sources, most notably Johnston, O'Malley, and Bachman (1992); and (d) *convenient compilations* of crime data found in the Department of Justice's annual *Sourcebook of Criminal Justice Statistics* (hereafter cited as *Sourcebook*).

5. Here the words *homicide* and *murder* are used interchangeably; technically speaking, however, homicide includes more than murder. We intend to follow the *Uniform Crime Reports*, which combines murder with nonnegligent homicides. This excludes negligent manslaughters, such as an automobile driver accidentally but negligently killing someone with his or her car. (For the technical uses and definitions of these and other words, see the 1991 *Sourcebook*, Appendix 3, or the *Uniform Crime Reports*.)

6. Each crime statistic is taken from the 1990 *Uniform Crime Reports*; for the number of major offenses and number of homicides, see Table 21; for methods and types of homicide (including romantic triangles and those involving narcotics felons) and total numbers and types of arrests, see Table 27.

7. The victim reports are compiled in the 1991 *Sourcebook*. See Table 3.1 and numerous tables following that.

8. Discussion of ordinary self-report data is based on statistics drawn from Johnston et al. (1992), which include high school students' use of alcohol, marijuana, and cocaine, including "ever used" and current use. The same statistics are covered in the 1991 *Sourcebook*, Tables 3.91 through 3.98. Student self-report of miscellaneous crimes is examined in Tables 3.77 through 3.90.

9. Quarrels leading to homicide are depicted on page 13 of the 1990 *Uniform Crime Reports*.

10. The number of justifiable homicides by police is presented in California Office of the Attorney General (1989). The 1991 updated data were obtained by telephone from Charlotte Rhe of the Bureau of Criminal Statistics and Special Services. There are also substantial data on police as victims of both homicides and assaults; see 1991 *Sourcebook*, Tables 3.159-3.164, 3.166-3.177. On the ordinariness of police work, see Moore (1992), especially pages 114-115. Also see Wycoff (1982).

11. For examples of current police shows on television, see the weekly television listings of your local newspaper or the weekly *TV Guide*.

12. For an example of large versus small newspaper coverage of crime, compare the daily "Security Roundup," in the *Daily Trojan*, the newspaper of the University of Southern California, to crime presented in the front and Metro sections of the daily *Los Angeles Times*.

13. Sherlock Holmes tales are anthologized in Doyle (1984). Examples of crime tales for television are in Hitchcock (1959), p. x.

14. For a description of the skilled thief of the past, see Sutherland (1956). Another important burglar study is by Bennett and Wright (1984).

15. See Cusson (1993). Be sure to compare with Sutherland (1956) and then compare both Cromwell and Cusson to Akerstrom (1993). See especially Chapter 4 on crime as work and Chapter 6 on social skills of offenders.

16. The ease of robbery is taken up in Bellot (1983); also see Gabor, Baril, Cusson, Elie, LeBlanc, and Normandeau (1987).

17. On the loose nature of most street gangs, see Klein (1971). For more misconceptions about gangs, see Klein, Maxson, and Cunningham (1991) and Maxson, Gordon, and Klein (1985).

18. Concerning exaggerations about organized crime, see Reuter (1984). On the basis for the organized crime myth making, consult Kappeler, Blumberg, and Potter (1993), pages 11-14.

19. On the age fallacy, see Chapter 6 of Gottfredson and Hirschi (1990). For age and victimization data, as well as victim reports of ages of assailants, see the 1991 *Sourcebook*, Table 3.33. Age arrest data are found in the 1990 *Uniform Crime Reports*, Table 27, and in the 1991 *Sourcebook*, Tables 4.3, 4.4, 4.5, 4.8, 4.9, 4.11, and 4.13.

20. For evidence that the age pattern for crime is offset by weapons ownership, see methods of murder on page 13 of the 1991 *Uniform Crime Reports*. Survey data on gun ownership by age are found in the 1991 *Sourcebook*, Tables 2.49 and 2.50.

21. Nonreporting of crime to the police is a central issue in reports of the National Crime Survey. See the 1991 *Sourcebook*, Tables 3.12 through 3.15. To verify police nondiscovery of most instances of illegal drug use, compare incidents of drug abuse from Johnston, O'Malley, and Bachman (1992) with arrests shown in Table 27 of the 1991 *Uniform Crime Reports*. Also see Gottfredson and Hirschi (1990) for how lack of opportunity to commit crime influences age data.

22. On delay in court, the days elapsing between arrest for larceny and conviction in state courts can be found in Table 5.52 of the 1991 *Sourcebook*. The statistics reported in the text include auto theft (not separated by the survey) and are based only on cases disposed of by trial. More modest statistics result if guilty pleas (which are far more numerous) are included. The median then becomes four months and the mean becomes six months.

23. On types of trials, see Table 5.48 of the 1991 *Sourcebook*, which documents the predominance of guilty pleas and bench trials.

24. Reinforcement schedules are covered in any introductory psychology textbook, but the special linkage to crime is thoroughly discussed in Gibbs (1975).

25. On the Kansas City Preventive Patrol Experiment, see Kelling, Pate, Dieckman, and Brown (1974). For research designed to help plan better patrols, see Larson (1972). A review of the patrol issue is found in Sherman (1983).

26. The number of sworn police officers per square mile of territory is from Table 1.35 in the 1989 *Sourcebook*. Los Angeles County's population and density are

from U.S. census as reported in the *World Almanac and Book of Facts, 1992* (New York: Pharos, 1991), page 110.

27. See Cohen and Felson (1979) for links between crime rates and prosperity. On the United States' highest homicide rate among developed countries, see U.S. Department of Justice (1988). When taken in a broader international perspective, including very high homicide rates in several less developed countries, the U.S. homicide rate does not look quite as bad; on this, see Brantingham and Brantingham (1984), Figure 10.1. About inconsistency and complexity of linkages between economics and crime, see Thornberry and Chriatiansen (1984) and Messner and Tardiff (1986). For doubts about links between inequality and crime rates, see Cohen and Felson (1979). Evidence that prosperous nations have high property crime rates is presented in Brantingham and Brantingham (1984), Figure 10-2, p. 254.

28. Sweden's crime wave is covered in Dolmen (1990). See also Wikstrom (1985).

29. On the liberal and conservative agendas, see Walker (1989). Also see Barlow (1990), pages 28-31 and 61-71. On crime for its own sake as the necessary focus, see Gottfredson and Hirschi (1990), especially Chapter 2.

30. On moralizing via social science, see Wrong (1961).

31. For a more extensive critique of the theories of crime in Table 1.2, see Chapter 1 of Hirschi (1969). Standard crime theories are found in the following sources. On *deterrence*, see Bentham (1948). On *incapacitation*, see Assembly of Behavioral and Social Sciences (1978). For a spirited and thoughtful attack on incapacitation policies, see Hirsch (1976). On *differential association*, see Cohen (1955) and Sutherland and Cressey (1974). For another approach, see Cloward and Ohlin (1960). On *labeling theory*, see Lemert (1972). On *strain theory*, see Merton (1957). On *control theory*, see Hirschi (1969). The insight of basic human frailty is a part of control theory. On *situational insight*, see Luckenbill (1970) plus references in Chapter 2. Check also Briar and Piliavin (1965). For entry into the social psychology literature on situations, see Bandura (1985). Also see Argyle, Furnham, and Graham (1981). The *temptation insight* is given more attention in Chapters 2 and 8; the latter provides references on reducing temptation to prevent crime. *Provocations* are discussed in Luckenbill (1970) and at greater length in Chapter 2. The *bad company insight* is an issue taken up in Chapter 1 of Hirschi (1969). Delinquency as a group activity is considered, for example, in Erickson and Jensen (1977), Reiss (1988), and Tremblay (forthcoming). The *idleness insight* is examined at great length in Hirschi (1969).

32. The tendency of some individuals to get in many types of trouble is a central issue in Gottfredson and Hirschi (1990). For an update with numerous additional references, see Grasmick, Tittle, Bursik, and Arneklev (1993), as well as Keane, Maxim, and Teevan (1993); the same issue of the *Journal of Research in Crime and Delinquency* has commentary from Gottfredson and Hirschi. On linkages among various "delinquencies," see Akers (1984); Hirschi (1969); Kandel (1978); Johnston, O'Malley, and Bachman (1992);

Hindelang, Hirschi, and Weis (1981); Schoff (1915); and Ferri (1897). On the nonspecialization of offenders, see Klein (1984).

33. On family problems and delinquency, see Sampson (1987). On social area analysis with family problems included, see Shaw and McKay (1931, 1942). For nuances about how families influence delinquency, see pages 97-105 in Gottfredson and Hirschi (1990).

34. Marriage "intactness" may miss the point in studying how strong families reduce crime. The problem is that "intact" families—those with a husband and wife still married—do not always provide a strong family life. Some "intact" families have a father or mother or both who are largely absent, while some single parents perform double duty, join with other single parents, or enlist other relatives to help deliver more adult time for children. Or, after separating, two parents may provide joint custody or regularly visit their children.

    Given that "intactness" is too crude and inaccurate to define or measure family strength, what better indicator can we find? We suggest that actual time that parents or other adult family members spend with children is a far better approach to defining family strength. Not denying that families can have a bad time together, we suggest that from a population viewpoint, more time means less crime.

    The issue of marriage intactness is considered in Hirschi (1983); that short chapter takes up several nuances about family life and crime. The time that families spend together is investigated by Medrich, Roizen, Rubin, and Buckley (1982).

35. The American legal system and its dealings with crime and criminals is very well reviewed in handbooks for lawyers and students produced for various states. A very good example is Katz (1987).

36. For arguments against criminals as a specific subset of the human race, see Fattah (1991), who includes review of details on the age and social composition of victims, which are in turn drawn from the United States' National Crime Survey and similar victim surveys in other nations.

37. That crime is not the province of a small segment of the population, see Gottfredson and Hirschi (1990).

2

The Chemistry for Crime

Routine is the god of every social system.

—*Alfred North Whitehead (Adventures in Ideas, 1933, p. 6)*

CONSCIENCE:
The inner voice which warns us
that someone is looking.

—*H. L. Mencken (A Book of Burlesques, 1916, p. 202)*

The following is the "Security Roundup" in the *Daily Trojan* for crimes reported to the University of Southern California's campus security for Monday, February 1, 1993:

- 11:00 a.m., a bulletin board was reportedly set on fire in Fluor Tower. The damage was minimal and there were no injuries reported.

- 11:20 a.m., a stereo and wallet were reported stolen from a garage at 701 W. 32nd St.

- 12:30 p.m., a bookbag was reported stolen from Crocker Library in Hoffman Hall.

- At 3:00 p.m., a robbery was reported at Hazard Park, located adjacent to the Health Sciences Campus. The suspect approached a student demanding money while simulating a gun in his pocket. The student complied, giving the suspect $10. The suspect fled and the student was not injured.

- At 11:50 p.m., a bike was reported stolen from 2821 Hoover St.

These five crimes were reported for a single day at a large urban university. Our task in this chapter is to examine these and other crime situations, breaking them down into their specific elements just as a chemist might analyze a molecule. Our chemistry for crime considers these types of crime: predatory crimes, illegal consumption, illegal sales, and fights.

Predatory Crimes

A predatory crime occurs when at least one person takes or damages the person or property of others.[1] All five crimes in the "Security Roundup" fit this category. Predatory crimes include those against persons and those against property owned by individuals or organizations. Among the crimes above, the robbery in Hazard Park is a violent crime against a person, whereas the thefts of stereo, wallet, bookbag, and bike are property crimes with individual victims. Setting the bulletin board afire is a crime against an organization (the University of Southern California, which owns Fluor Tower). For a predatory crime to occur, law or custom must define personal or property rights clearly so that we can tell whether one person treads on the rights of another. For example, the stereo in the garage on 32nd Street belongs to someone besides the thief, and the robber in Hazard Park had no right to threaten the student.

Predatory crime incidents depend on the physical convergence of these three elements:

+ a likely offender,
+ a suitable target, and
+ the absence of capable guardians.

Note that the predatory crime situation has two presences and one absence: An offender and a target converge in the absence of a guardian against the crime. We turn first to an explanation of targets of crime.

Crime Targets

A target of crime is defined from the viewpoint of the specific crime as it is carried out at a specific location and time. For example, the offender's target may be a wallet. The offender has a practical problem: to get to the wallet and remove it or its contents from the scene of the crime. In most offenses, the offender does not even know who the wallet belongs to and does not much care.[2] In the case of the stereo, wallet, bookbag, and bike in the "Security Roundup," the crime victim's property was targeted in his or her absence. With the robbery in Hazard Park, the offender targeted a student and the student's money. When the student gave him the $10, the offender fortunately lost interest in the student as a target and fled. Each crime occurred with guardians absent.

Guardians Against Crime

The word *guardian* makes many people think of police officers, who are very unlikely to be on the spot when a crime occurs. The most significant guardians in society are ordinary citizens going about their daily routines. Usually you are the best guardian for your own property. Your friends and relatives also can serve as guardians for your person and property, as you can for theirs. Even strangers can serve as guardians by being nearby and thus discouraging offenders. A guardian discourages offenders from attempting to carry out an offense in the first place.[3] This same principle applies to illegal consumption, as the next section shows.

Illegal Consumption and Sales

Illegal consumption (including illegal drug consumption and underage drinking) is another important example of criminal behavior. Although illegal consumption generally occurs in groups, for simplicity we now discuss a "solo crime," namely, those situations in which someone uses or consumes substances alone. This seems to be such a simple crime, but is it? Each solo offense involves the presence of one offender, but it also depends on the absence of anyone to interfere.[4] For example, a teenager smoking a marijuana joint at home alone normally depends on the absence of parents or anybody else who would prevent the crime from occurring. Even a stranger such as a deliveryman might ring the doorbell, or a casual acquaintance such as a neighbor might stop by. The offender may feel impelled to quit the crime and hide the joint. So a solo crime depends on many people!

Although we began with solo crimes, most illegal consumption involves at least two offenders in the absence of guardians. Both predatory crimes and illegal consumption depend on some presences and some absences. It is generally the absences that complicate criminal events by linking them to the routine activities of the rest of society. When these activities bring guardians around to the wrong place at the wrong time (from the offender's point of view), they serve to prevent crime from happening. When these activities keep guardians away, they make crime more likely.

Of course, converging presences are also important. For example, illegal consumption is more likely to occur when two or more youths so inclined converge in the absence of guardians. Their offense is collaborative, and they have a joint incentive to avoid detection.

This incentive is also evident with illegal sales, which include illegal sales of sexual services, drugs, alcohol to minors, and the like. These sales involve an illegal buyer and an illegal seller, acting in different roles and thus symbiotically violating the law.[5]

In the next section, we discuss a type of crime with a more complicated chemistry.

Fights and Their
Antecedent Arguments

A man named Jose is currently housed in the prison system of New York state. Here is the verbatim description from the Department of Correctional Services of the event that got him there:

> During the evening of April 16, 1976, approximately 11:45 p.m., the defendant was standing in the street with a group of other men, all imbibing alcoholic beverages near 1318 Southern Blvd. Meanwhile, nearby other groups of people were similarly engaged. The deceased (Angel), who had been a member of one of those groups, hurled an emptied whiskey bottle into the air which crashed at the feet of the defendant, dirtying the latter's trousers. At this point, the defendant, who had been acquainted with the deceased, approached the deceased complaining of the latter's actions. Momentarily the deceased picked up a stick and he began hitting the defendant with it about the legs. Fleeing, the defendant ran into his apartment and locked his front door. However, the deceased, who had pursued the defendant remained just outside the defendant's door, taunting him and challenging him to come out.
>
> After some minutes, when the defendant felt that the deceased was no longer standing in front of his door, he left his apartment and returned to the street. Once in the street, the defendant again confronted the deceased and they resumed their verbal argument which also included some pushing and shoving.
>
> Within moments the defendant grabbed a baseball bat which had been nearby and wielding it over his head, struck the deceased with it on the top and side of his scalp, grievously wounding him.[6]

This homicide would not make much of a television show, but it is fairly typical. Both men were drinking and insulting, arguing, pushing, shoving, and hitting one another. There was plenty of blame to go around. So police officers followed the usual procedure: They took the man who won the fight to jail and the man who lost the fight to a hospital (and later to the morgue). To learn more about how fights occur, we need to learn something about arguments.

How Arguments Are Provoked

University researchers have added to our knowledge about conflict by provoking arguments in social psychology laboratories. These studies have many variants, but the general form is this:

> Subject Y, working for the researcher, sits down in the room and pretends to be a subject.

> The real subject of the research, Subject X, is invited in to the room and sits down.

> The researcher leaves the room and watches what happens through a one-way screen so that Subject X does not know he or she is still watching.

> Suddenly Subject Y insults Subject X. For example, Subject Y might say to Subject X, "That's sure an ugly shirt you're wearing." The research question is whether Subject X ignores the insult, answers in kind, or escalates with a worse insult.

Research of this form varies several conditions:

- the age of Subject X,
- the age of Subject Y,
- an audience,
- the presence of a troublemaker (e.g., saying to Subject X, "You aren't going to let him say that to you, are you?"), and
- the presence of a peacemaker (e.g., saying to Subject X, "Just ignore that").

The goal of this research is to determine the situations in which subjects answer insults and escalate the consequences. This research finds that subjects are more likely to respond and escalate when there is an audience present to hear the insult; they tend to ignore more insults when no one else is present. The research also finds strong age and sex components in the response to insults. For example, a male youth insulted by a middle-aged woman will tend to shrug it off. But a male youth insulted by another male youth in front of other male youths will tend not to shrug it off; he is likely to respond with his own insult and even to escalate the conflict. In addition, subjects return the insult and escalate more often when a troublemaker is present and egging them on. They return the insult and escalate less often when a peacemaker is present to calm them down. With alcohol in the bloodstream, subjects return the insult and escalate more often.[7]

Together these findings imply that assembling young males increases the chance for arguments to occur and escalate, especially if alcohol is present. In contrast, mixing sexes and ages tends to reduce the chances that arguments will ensue.

From a Small Argument Grows a Bad Fight

These principles extracted by laboratory research also apply to the "real world." Fights typically occur among groups of young males, often after drinking alcohol in bars or elsewhere. Most fights start with an insult or perceived insult by one party. This may lead to a response in kind, an escalation of aggressive words, and finally to a fight. As we saw with Jose above, even a homicide can result from such an argument. Indeed, in 1990 more than one half of U.S. homicides that were not committed in the context of other felonies arose from simple arguments.

We can state these basic elements for a fight:

- combatants,
- troublemakers,
- audience, and
- the absence of peacemakers.

A fight requires two or more combatants to converge in space and time. It is most likely to occur if these combatants also converge with an audience and troublemakers in the absence of peacemakers.

We have described the chemistry for four types of crime. Although some types of crime have not been covered, these examples illustrate a general approach to the chemistry for crime: Figure out who must be present and who must be absent for a crime to occur. The next sections discuss several additional physical attributes that we must understand for their addition to this chemistry.

Diverse Physical Requirements of Criminal Incidents

This section examines several physical traits that contribute to more or less crime. We begin with articles that are most easily stolen.

Weight and Mobility of Goods

Physical features of property targets are very important for producing or preventing predatory crime. For example, lists of articles often reported as stolen include such items as television sets, videocassette recorders, portable computers, stereo components, compact disc players, car stereos, jewelry, bicycles, automobiles, accessories attached to automobiles, and packages left in automobiles.

Of central importance for becoming a target of predatory property crime is the value of the target proportional to its weight.[8] This was evident in the "Security Roundup" at the beginning of the chapter. Items stolen included a wallet, a bookbag, and a stereo: All are high in value per pound. For example, check the weight per pound of the items listed in a Sears catalog and compare with lists of most commonly stolen items. Consider a specific example: Washing machines are worth several hundred dollars, but only about $4 per pound. They are seldom stolen. In contrast, electronic consumer goods are high in value per pound and are highly attractive targets of crime. This same idea has been used to predict the annual burglary rate in the United States since 1947 from the lightest television set in the Sears catalog for each year.

The weight of goods is not the only determinant of their tendency to be stolen. Vehicles provide their own getaway and thus are more suitable for theft than their weight would indicate. This explains the presence of bicycles and automobiles on the list of most commonly stolen goods. An interesting illustration is offered by a family that had three bicycles sitting in its garage. When the family returned from vacation, two of the three bicycles were stolen—but because the best bicycle had no air in its tires, it had been left untouched.

Physical aspects are important not only for crime production but also for crime prevention. Although Chapter 8 is devoted entirely to the study of crime prevention, the next section introduces some prevention ideas that illustrate crime as a physical phenomenon.

Physical Crime Prevention

Crime can be prevented by at least three physical methods: target hardening, construction, and strength in numbers.

Examples of target hardening are found around universities when they bolt down computers, typewriters, television sets, projection equipment, and the like.[9]

To reduce their vulnerability to theft, organizations and individuals sometimes construct walls, fences, and other physical barriers to prevent illegal entry or exit or simply to channel flows of people coming and going and thus make mild supervision possible.[10] For example, the University of Southern California put a fence around the premises in preparation for the 1984 Olympic games. The campus was still open at many gates, but offenders could no longer enter anywhere, attack anything or anyone, and exit anywhere afterward.

Like offenders, victims can enhance their position by strength in numbers. In the 1990 National Crime Survey, 16% of robbery victims reported being robbed by multiple offenders, but almost all reported being the sole victim. Numbers clearly provide some measure of safety for both men and women.[11]

Sights and Sounds Affecting Crime

People who flash large wads of money are inviting crime victimization. Conversely, stores that hide their cash-counting operations in an upstairs office gain some protection by not tempting people needlessly. Being out of sight helps protect some illegal transactions from the prying eyes of the community. Visibility helps to explain why automobile accessories and contents are at such a high risk of theft.[12]

Sound is also important for crime. Better locks on homes are important not so much to prevent burglars from entering (because most locks are fairly easy to break) but to make sure that offenders make enough noise to draw the attention of others. Alarm systems operate on the same principle. Noisy dogs can serve both to alert others and to scare off offenders directly. Noise can also be directed at offenders, as when subway station personnel with loudspeakers direct someone to cease an undesirable behavior. Offenders may bang on doors to ascertain whether people are home or otherwise help them make decisions about when or where to act illegally. In these ways, sound serves as a physical means of crime prevention or as a way to carry it out.

Dangerous Places, Risky Routes, and Unassigned Space

Research by Dennis Roncek on "dangerous places" has shown that those city blocks that contain a bar or a public high school are significantly more likely to have burglaries and other property crimes. Other work on dangerous places by Lawrence Sherman shows that a small number of addresses (such as a tough bar or drug house) generate many more than their share of calls for police service. Even within a so-called dangerous neighborhood, many addresses appear to be quite safe, while others are quite unsafe.[13]

Paul and Pat Brantingham have plotted property crimes in one town with respect to proximity to a McDonald's restaurant, which draws many youths in early crime-prone ages.[14] They have also found that places near a city's "rough bar" suffer more property crime.

The Brantinghams have elaborated on this to describe the "geometry of crime." The description follows these steps:

1. Find out first where each potential offender (a) lives, (b) works or goes to school, and (c) engages in leisure.

2. Trace the routes among these three places to form a triangle.

3. Trace a block or two off of these routes to form a triangular search space.

This description provides the area within which the offender searches for crime targets. Offenders may travel a few streets off the main routes, but in general they do not wander much farther looking for crime targets. Like anybody else, they stick close to the streets they know. Indeed, offenders will neglect very suitable crime targets that are not on the routes they know.[15]

Offenders are also especially likely to commit crimes along well-traveled routes, while out-of-the-way locations escape their attention. A fascinating Canadian study by Dan Beavon of an area near Vancouver, British Columbia, tells us a lot about how physical street patterns relate to crime risk.[16]

Figure 2.1a shows a street block with House X. One other street turns into this block, which then ends in a cul-de-sac (marked by the zero). In contrast, Figure 2.1b shows six other streets turning into the block with House Y.

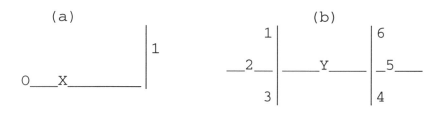

Figure 2.1 Physical Street Patterns and Risk of Crime

By counting the number of turns into each block, Beavon found a correlation of more than .95 between the number of streets turning into a block and its property crime rate. This is a very high correlation for criminology. It tells us that House X in Figure 2.1a will have a very low property crime risk, while House Y in Figure 2.1b will have a very high risk. This demonstrates that inconvenient access reduces what convenient access produces: more crime. This also helps explain why a vast grid of wide and sweeping boulevards helps to produce crime, however desirable it may be for moving automobiles quickly.

Boulevards are also important for producing vast swaths of space that escape natural social controls. They fit into a larger system as follows. Think of a city's space along the continuous scale shown in Figure 2.2.

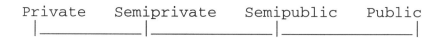

Figure 2.2 Continuum of Physical Space

On the left is completely private space, such as a person's home, a fenced school, and a government facility that does not admit people. Note that some private space is publicly owned and that privacy is defined by limited access. On the right is completely public space, such as a shopping center, a wide boulevard, a college campus, and a large public park. Note that some privately owned places have complete public access, while some publicly owned places do not permit public access for those who have no business there. In general, crime is most easily committed in places with complete public access (on the right of the scale) and it is most difficult to commit in places with private access (on the left of the scale).[17]

The middle of the scale is the most interesting part. For example, a very large housing complex with fences and many unlocked gates is semiprivate, inhibiting access only partially. Semipublic space is exemplified by small local streets. As Jane Jacobs recognized in 1961, small streets are subject to neighborly supervision and quiet crime prevention. Residents treat the sidewalk and street in front of their own homes as their responsibility, even if the ownership of the space is public.

A general crime prevention strategy in urban settings is to plan the use of space. This means making as much space as possible private, semiprivate, or semipublic. Thus parks and streets should not be too large, and public housing should not have vast unassigned spaces.

We have talked about design of space but not about what people actually do. Now we turn to activity patterns that reduce victimization risks.

Family and Household Settings

In terms of crime victimization, time spent in family and household settings is less risky than time spent away from these settings. Because people spend so much time with families and at home, such settings produce many victimizations for this reason alone. Indeed, violent incidents reported in the National Crime Survey are about equally likely to be at or very near home as in other settings.[18] However, when controlling for the time spent in various settings, each hour spent on public streets and conveyances turns out to be at least 10 times more risky than an hour spent at home. It is clearly not very risky to be home per hour spent there, and those people who spend more time in nonhousehold, nonfamily settings have a much higher risk of crime victimization. Table 2.1 shows the major victimization risks.[19]

Table 2.1 Major Victimization Risks

Persons at Higher Risk	Persons at Lower Risk
Youths	Elderly
Males	Females
Single persons	Married persons
Those living alone	Those living with others
Those in the labor force or school	Those keeping house

Thus young males who are single, living alone, and either in school or the labor force are several times more likely to be victimized than are older married females who keep house and live with others. Victim studies consistently support the patterns just noted. Moreover, they establish that one household of six people has less household victimization than six households of one person each. This point applies not only to personal victimizations but also household victimizations, such as burglary, household larceny, and auto theft. In other words, a car owned by someone living alone is more likely to be stolen than a car owned by someone living with other persons. We suggest that those who live alone are more likely to go out at night and thus park their cars on streets that expose them to theft. In general, nonfamily and nonhousehold activities often occur in dangerous places near offenders but away from likely guardians against crime.

In applying this analysis, be sure to consider both family and household together. Leaving home with family members to go to family restaurants is not very risky. Leaving home and family to go to tough bars dominated by hard drinkers is much riskier. On the other hand, leaving youths home alone creates a nonfamily household setting, minimizing social control and producing crime opportunities. The next section takes up related physical aspects of social control.

Informal Social Control of Youth: Physical Aspects

An important source of information on control is Travis Hirschi's control theory, which focuses on the social bond between youths and society as a means of preventing delinquency. Its basic hypothesis is that delinquency is reduced by tying youths into society. This is accomplished when:

* strong attachments to parents and family lead youths to avoid the disgrace that results from being caught in delinquent acts;

* strong commitments to future goals (such as graduating from high school and going to college) lead youths to avoid being caught in delinquent acts; and

* youths simply become so busy with conventional activities that they have no time left for delinquent behavior.

Suppose, for example, that a certain teenager does not care what parents think, has no plans for the future, and is not very busy. Social control is lacking, and delinquency may well occur. Conversely, a boy or girl with strong bonds to parents, a commitment to attend college, and a very busy school and extracurricular life would tend to avoid delinquency.

However, control theory only presents part of the information we need to understand the informal control of youths in an urban or suburban society. Consider these points:

* It is easy to drive the car somewhere to avoid parents and teachers, to commit a delinquent act free from control.

* Crime in modern society has become easy to commit with little risk of getting caught; so society cannot deliver control anyway.

* Thus it is possible to mesh illegal behavior with conventional roles such as jobs (see Chapter 5), schooling (see Chapter 6), or afterschool activities (see Chapter 7).

In short, it is possible to have your social bonds and be delinquent too.

Physical Convergences

The chemistry for crime leads us to conclude for the larger society that a higher crime rate can occur without more offenders. For example, predatory crimes can increase if the same number of offenders can find more targets for crime in the absence of guardians against crime. Illegal consumption and sales can increase with more evasion of guardians. Fights can increase if likely combatants converge more often in the presence of an audience and a troublemaker and in the absence of a peacemaker.

Each crime has its particular chemistry. Crimes also have a common chemistry, because a situation in which young males have no adults present implies a risk of higher crime rates of all types.

The chemistry of crime leads us to consider its physics as everyday life assembles the elements going into each crime and noncrime situation. This is why we can call this the *routine activity approach* to crime analysis.[20] This approach emphasizes how illegal activities feed on routine legal activities in the context of everyday life. These routines deliver temptations and controls and thus organize the type and amount of crime in society. The next chapter considers some historical changes that influence how routines change and thus affect crime rates.

Questions for Writing, Reflection, and Debate

---

1. Several types of crime were mentioned in this chapter. Discuss what they have in common, as well as what differs among them. Are there any types of crime not covered? What are their elements?

2. Use the routine activity approach to name three specific places near you that are especially safe from crime and three others that are especially dangerous. Explain why and defend your list.

3. What are society's various lines of defense against crime? Name as many as you can think of and then evaluate their relative effectiveness.

Sources for Ideas

For a thorough study of crime from the viewpoint of the victim, see Fattah (1991). This volume provides easy entrée into many ideas about how people become victims of crime and how crime rates change. It also helps to develop an image of the criminal similar to that presented in these first two chapters.

Additional ideas about crime are presented in the essay "The Ecology of Crime" (Felson, 1983), which explains how crime feeds on the larger environment and uses that idea to classify different types of crime. The article also explains that crime can kill the very environment it feeds on, such as a vice-driven skid row area whose crime rate gets so high that it drives out the very illegal business on which it feeds.

This chapter did not get into specifying the roles in organized crime activities, a topic that is nicely covered in Reuter's *Disorganized Crime* (1984). Pages 20-25 of that text describe the four roles for illegal bookmaking and sports betting: bettor, runner, clerk, and bookmaker; pages 47-53 discuss the specific participants in the numbers racket; and page 94 discusses the simpler organization of loan sharking.

Endnotes

1. For details on minimal elements of predatory crimes, see Cohen and Felson (1979). Original work on predatory crime is found in Glaser (1971), page 4.

2. For excellent details on specific property targeted for property crime, see Illinois Law Enforcement Commission (1984 and annually thereafter). However, the most recent issue of this document (now from the Illinois State Police) unfortunately removes many of these interesting details.

3. On guardianship, see Newman (1972) and Jacobs (1961).

4. Extensive and interesting evidence connects solo crime and suicide. See compiled evidence of Clarke and Lester (1989) and Clarke and Mayhew (1988).

5. For an overall study on illegal markets, see Reuter (1984). On the connection of drugs with crime, see Tonry and Morris (1990). For a study of prostitution as a tangible activity, see Lowman (1986). On underage drinking, note the status offense data in the 1989 *Sourcebook*, Tables 5.96 through 5.100.

6. The description of the incident on April 16, 1976, was provided by New York state's Department of Correctional Services and is a matter of public record.

7. On situational aspects of fights and violence and for reviews of the situational literature, consult Luckenbill (1977, pp. 176-186), Felson and Steadman (1983, pp. 59-74), and Felson (1993).

8. Weight and mobility of goods as related to crime are detailed in Cohen and Felson (1979). See also Felson and Cohen (1981; as corrected 1982).

9. Target hardening is exemplified by Ekblom (1992) and Decker (1992), both in the same collection.

10. Construction for preventing crime largely originates with work by Newman (1972). See also Poyner (1983) and Poyner and Webb (1991). In Chapter 8, we discuss this issue further.

11. On strength in numbers, see *Sourcebook* (1989), Tables 3.51-3.60; on weapons use, see Table 3.63.

12. On lines of sights and sound, see the review of convenience store crime prevention in Hunter and Jeffery (1992) and Duffala (1972). These studies are discussed further in Chapter 8.

13. For research on dangerous places, see Roncek and Maier (1991), Roncek and Lobosco (1983), and Sherman, Gartin, and Buerger (1989).

14. The work on crime and proximity to McDonald's is found in Brantingham and Brantingham (1982).

15. For information on how offenders search for crime targets along the routes they know, see Chapter 1 in Brantingham and Brantingham (1990).

16. See Beavon (1984), which explores street patterns in crime. These ideas also can be traced back to Bevis and Nutter (1977).

17. The discussion of private and public space goes back to Jacobs (1961). An interesting consideration of the same issue is found in Rapoport (1977), pages 288-298. Privatizing space is further discussed in Coleman (1985).

18. Links between victimization and marital and living arrangements are detailed in Hindelang, Gottfredson, and Garafolo (1978).

19. Tying informal social control into the physical world draws its ideas from Hirschi (1969) and is explained in greater detail in Felson (1986). Calculations of risks both at and away from home are reported in Cohen and Felson (1979). These relationships are found in many *Sourcebook* tables drawn from the National Crime Survey.

20. Felson (1983) presents a more abstract examination of the points in this chapter.

3

The Convergent City: More Crime Than Towns

People are trapped in history
and history is trapped in them.

—James Baldwin
("Stranger in the Village," 1953, in Notes of a Native Son, 1955)

The form and content of man's collective life
is a function of the efficiency of his means
of transportation and communication.

—Amos Hawley
(Urban Society: An Ecological Approach, 1971, p. v)

The first two chapters worked toward two goals. Chapter 1 showed that individuals are highly responsive to temptations and controls. Chapter 2 examined how temptations and controls apply to specific crime situations and their avoidance. But neither chapter told us much about how people or things get to the scene of the crime. Chapter 3 considers how society delivers temptation and control. We are using the word *deliver* literally, examining changes in transport systems for people and goods as they influence crime in everyday life.

What Changes and What Remains Constant?

To understand what changes, we have to specify what does not change at all. First, let us assume that people will forever meet and talk face-to-face, no matter how far technology develops. Second, we note that people continue to walk every day within a limited area, even as transportation systems become more advanced. In sum, people as we know them walk a little and talk a lot and will forever do so.

What changes is how society sets up that walking and talking. New technology plays the central role in delivering people to one another in entirely different mixes and from entirely different distances. Thus telephones help people make dates over quite a bit of space, and transportation machinery helps them keep those dates. Once together, they interact in the old-fashioned way.

The effect of communication and transportation systems is to alter who meets, when they meet, how long they travel to meet on a daily basis, and how wide the physical span of movement is for people who meet. These changes in turn generate different opportunities for crime to occur. To find out how daily life contributes to more crime or less, we need to know how people and goods move about in the course of a day.[1] More specifically, we need to ask:

* Where do people live and who lives together?
* Where and when do people work or otherwise interact?
* What goods exist and where are they stored?
* How and when do people and goods move around?

The answers to these questions relate to society's energy and transportation systems.

Hawley's Four Stages
in the History of Everyday Life

An excellent account of the powerful impact of changing energy and transportation systems on human history is found in Professor Amos Hawley's *Urban Society: An Ecological Approach* (1971). The man responsible for systematizing modern human ecology, Hawley traces human history in terms of the use of nonhuman energy, settlement patterns, and the structure of daily interaction. Table 3.1 shows his timeline of human history, which we have modified to help analyze how crime changes in the course of history.

The timeline shows Hawley's four historical stages in this order: (A) village, (B) town, (C) urban, and (D) metropolitan. Each stage depicts a system of everyday life. From the first to the fourth stages, dramatic changes occur in everyday life and the crime that feeds on it. These changes are fed by a shift (Line 1) from reliance on human muscle to use

Table 3.1 Hawley's Four Stages in the History of Everyday Life

	Stage			
Traits	A. Village	B. Town	C. Urban	D. Metro
1. Nonhuman energy	animal	animal, water, wind	fossil	fossil, electric, nuclear
2. Nonpedestrian local travel	none	horse	street rail	automobile
3. Daily radius of activity (miles)	4	8	12	50
4. Daily dependence on proximity	exclusive	substantial	moderate	minimal
5. Local population size	250	15,000	100,000	250,000+
6. Nonfarm population (%)	2	20	40	60+
7. Rural banditry	serious	moderate	minimal	minimal
8. Local crime	minimal	limited	serious	endemic

Source: Adapted from Hawley (1971), Table 59, p. 325.

of modern fuels, this producing a 200-fold increase in productivity per worker over the four stages. Line 2 shows a shift in local travel, which is entirely on foot in the first stage and involves automobiles in the last stage. This transforms the radius of daily activity and interaction (Line 3) from 4 miles in the first stage to 50 miles in the last stage, in turn greatly reducing the daily dependence on proximity (Line 4). At first, everyday life depends exclusively on proximity; in time, proximity becomes less important as transportation allows people to go long distances on a daily basis.

Local population size (Line 5) increases from 250 people to 250,000 or more. The nonfarm population (Line 6) rises from 2% of the total population to 60% or more. In short, we see everyday life transformed from a small-scale to a large-scale system.

These changes in turn influence the amount of two types of crime: highway bandits and raids (Line 7) and local crime within settlements (Line 8). Now we deal with the same timeline column by column.

The Village Stage

As Column A indicates, the village uses only animal energy to supplement human energy. With beasts of burden pulling a plow but local travel on foot, the population's daily radius of activity is only some four miles. Except for a few administrative cities, this permits an approximate local population of only 250 people, and almost everyone is involved in farming. In such a setting, daily interaction is based exclusively on proximity, and everyday work is carried out mostly in kinship groups. Trading involves mostly nearby villages and a few long-distance travelers. Strangers could seldom assemble in large numbers.

Within the small scale of village life, people know a good deal about one another. If one person steals something from another, the theft is very difficult to conceal. Not only would the thief be seen, but custom-made utensils and products are easy to recognize when in the hands of someone other than the owner. It is very difficult to carry out secret criminal acts within the village itself. However, the village era is plagued by highway robbery, raids by marauding bandits or between villages.[2]

The Town Stage

The domestication of the horse and the use of water and wind power make possible the next stage of daily organization, the town. As Column B indicates, this system expands the distance of daily interaction to some eight miles and local populations to approximately 15,000 people. The nonfarm share of the population increases to as much as 20%. Proximity is no longer the exclusive basis for organizing daily interaction, but it is still dominant. The shift from village to town makes possible a 10-fold increase in the nonfarm share of the population and a 60-fold increase in total size of local settlements.

Although some townspeople might not know one another by name, most would recognize one another or have a mutual friend or relative. The proximity of daily interaction continues to make mild supervision of youths the rule, and it keeps guardianship against local crime strong.

The widespread use of horses transforms the stakes of crime and anticrime activities, because both raiders and soldiers can now conduct speedy raids. Horses and wagons help assemble more goods in fewer places, making better targets for crime. Horses themselves provide a new target of theft and with a quick getaway. With incremental improvements in boats and barges, more goods are assembled into a single place, providing better targets for crime. For example, writing in 1796 about London's crime wave, Patrick Colquhoun emphasized the vast increase in goods flowing through London's wharves and warehouses. These goods themselves provided an extra invitation to theft, while the added commerce helped to augment the population. Not only are residents of a larger settlement more often strangers to one another, but strangers from elsewhere are more likely to enter for commercial purposes. As fewer people recognize one another, informal social control weakens and local crime grows. As larger settlements develop, local areas of great danger emerge, from the rookeries of London to the tough neighborhoods of Philadelphia.[3] Such cities and urban problems emerge before the urban era itself takes hold. That era has yet to transform the nature of crime.

The Urban Stage

Fossil fuels feed the growth of more and bigger cities. As Column C in the timeline indicates, these fuels make possible streetcars and thus a common expansion of cities to cover 12 miles and to include 100,000 persons. Nonfarm population may increase to 40%, and immediate proximity becomes less essential for organizing daily activities. Railroads concentrate goods in central locations, producing more targets of theft. Steam-powered factories assemble larger numbers of workers on different shifts at all hours of day and night. With more goods and more strangers comes a turning point in the history of crime location: Crime is now a routine problem of urban life.

Improved engines and brakes make it easier for trains and streetcars to accelerate and stop, picking up more passengers at more stops and delivering them quickly between home and work. Electric engines avoid the soot and smoke of steam engines, permitting the construction of underground transportation systems. Meanwhile, elevators help cities grow vertically. The result is a much higher population density and vastly more daily contact among strangers.

A new urban crime pattern emerges as the city grows, with predatory offenders hiding in the crowd, attacking, and then hiding again to evade apprehension. Illegal sales and consumption as well as fights can more readily survive within an urban setting. As cities grew larger, something new develops: the convergent city. Such a city offers employers a large labor force ready to converge at a single factory or office building, using the same assembly line, equipment, or files; dealing with the same customers and suppliers; and supervised and coordinated by on-the-spot bosses.

Manhattan as a Living Remnant of the Convergent City

Many Americans born after 1960 have never gone downtown to shop. Even people older than 40 may have forgotten what cities were like, so we will describe a living example: the borough of Manhattan in New York City. Even though the era of the convergent city has passed for most of the nation, it seems to live on in Manhattan.[4]

Crowds and Heights

Manhattan is packed with skyscrapers. The people who live there must pay tremendous prices for tiny apartments, and stores must pay exorbitant rent for slivers of commercial space. Grocery stores are a tiny fraction of the size of their counterparts in the rest of the country. Crowds of people get off work in the evening, packing the sidewalks like people exiting a Big Ten football game. Most stores thrive without the need to advertise, simply drawing from the crowds of people walking by. Great varieties of restaurants and other shops cater to the diverse population and take advantage of the pedestrian crowds. Baked goods have no time to get stale because the flow of customers buys them so quickly; the pleasant aromas of fresh goods mixes with the stench from what these same pedestrians toss into the streets.[5]

Transport System

The map of subway and commuter train lines shows that almost all routes from the other four boroughs of New York City and from three states lead into Manhattan like the spokes of a wheel. New Jersey Transit trains and PATH subways, commuter trains from Long Island and Connecticut, commuter boats from New Jersey and Staten Island, greater New York subway lines—all lead into Manhattan. This vast system funnels millions of people from the surrounding residential areas through the transport corridors into Manhattan in the morning, then out again in the evening. Shopping and extra activities fill in the cracks, which are found near work, near home, and along the fixed transport corridors between the two. In sum, work and home form a bipolar system, with the daily cycle of life shifting back and forth between the poles.

Train corridors impose a special discipline on everyday life. Train routes are inflexible. Citizens plan their daily life around the train's fixed stops, taking into account how far they are willing to walk. Stores have to be within walking distance, and customers only buy what they can carry. Thus many people purchase fresh groceries daily in small amounts from small stores. These pedestrians enrich neighborhood life and keep neighborhood stores and institutions alive. However, Manhattan is by no means a perfect fossil of the convergent city.

Differences Between Manhattan
and Previous Convergent Cities

Manhattan was never the perfect representative of the American convergent city.[6] Its population has always been larger, its buildings higher, and its transport system more complicated. Other convergent cities in the United States housed most people in duplexes, triplexes, row houses, and apartment buildings of a few stories rather than Manhattan-styled skyscrapers. New York's borough of Brooklyn is more similar than Manhattan to the other old cities of the United States.[7]

Like other U.S. urban areas, Manhattan's population density has declined in recent decades as residences, shopping, and jobs shifted to the suburbs. Many people who continue to work in Manhattan enter and leave by automobile. A highway system has joined the public transit system to bring in commuters in the morning and send them home in the evening. Yet Manhattan provides a good example of some aspects of the historic convergent city and its social control patterns. To understand these patterns, we need to learn more about the physiology of the convergent city.

The Organs of the Convergent City

The convergent city has six major organs:

1. a central business district (CBD),
2. an entertainment district,
3. an industrial district (including delinquency areas),
4. transportation corridors,
5. households, and
6. urban villages.

The first three are "central" districts and are discussed in this section.[8]

Central Districts

The central business district (CBD) is truly the heart of the convergent city. It is the center of work and shopping, as well as the place to which the transport system feeds people. It is characterized by a huge daytime population, but it is largely abandoned at night and on weekends, except for a special entertainment district, carved in or near the CBD, which thrives during these same times. An industrial district beside or around the CBD contains factories and warehouses that provide many jobs. This district may have both a nighttime and a daytime population, because many factories run 24 hours each day.

Delinquency Areas

Although many of the central districts lack a residential population, there is an important exception. As Shaw and McKay wrote earlier this century, the city has delinquency areas within the central districts that usually straddle the industrial zone. These areas are characterized by very high rates of residential turnover, low rates of home ownership, and substantial amounts of family disruption. Here reside the poorest, the newest immigrants, and relatively more disrupted families. The high crime rates of these areas persist over many decades, even as ethnic composition changes. This disorganization in delinquency areas combines many social problems, including higher numbers of psychotic people and higher rates of infectious disease, alcoholism, truancy, school problems, and unemployment. These delinquency areas may also include a skid row on which downward mobility has reached rock-bottom and social disorganization is extreme. These central districts are linked to the rest of the convergent city by the transport system.

Transportation Corridors

The circulatory organ of the convergent city is its transportation system. This not only includes various types of trains—streetcars, subways, and commuter trains—but also their stations, connecting buses, and bus stops. Even more relevant are the sidewalks that transport pedestrians to and from the stations and bus stops and then into and out of the vehicles of mass transport. Just as human blood flows from the heart through the arteries to the capillaries, so the circulatory system of the convergent city is a series of corridors. People flow through this circulatory system via trains along their tracks to stations, from stations onto sidewalks, along sidewalks to bus stops, from bus stops onto buses via streets, off again onto bus stops and sidewalks, and back again.

This transport system is at the core of the crime problem for the convergent system. It distributes crowds of strangers, exposing them to limited social control. It provides places to hang out, with temptations high, controls low, and quick exits provided to offenders. Yet it also provides sufficient numbers of pedestrians to offer guardians against the most extreme forms of violent attack. Chapter 7 discusses at length how urban streets and central districts contribute to and yet put some limits on crime.[9]

It is evident why the convergent city has less control and therefore more crime within it than a village or town. However, the history of crime and security is also a history of trial and error. As the convergent city develops, organs for social control evolve with it.

Social Control and Crime Prevention in Convergent Cities

A city is not merely a mass of people in central districts and transport corridors; it is a body that also develops smaller organs, namely, households and neighborhoods.

Households

Some patterns of crime are easier to spot if we think of natural analogs. One of these is the nest, where an animal seeks to protect itself and its offspring from predators.[10] Human households are similar. There people store the product of their labor and shelter their families.

In the general convergent city we describe, relatively few women are in the labor force, and families are large. Deaths and separations lead to fusing of families rather than movement into separate households. As a result, households include not only more members of the immediate family, but also other relatives and boarders. In the convergent city, women remain at or near home most of the time, providing households with a daytime population.

The Urban Village

Homes in the convergent city are apartments, row houses, or houses on very small lots. Proximity produces a natural community life. Women provide a sufficient daytime population of adults in the residential neighborhood. They talk to one another in hallways and over fences, providing a natural street life as well. Lacking automobiles, women purchase goods locally and participate in local institutions, such as churches and voluntary associations. Even if the convergent city has many strangers, its local people often know one another by name or sight. Ethnic homogeneity in many urban neighborhoods contributes to localism. For example, if most people in a given neighborhood speak Italian and look Italian, someone not Italian will be recognized as an outsider. Although prejudices might have been strong among many groups, within each group there is a sense of responsibility for the local area. Together these factors contribute a practical basis for local community plus a sense of belonging—an urban village.[11] This localism assists city people to maximize control and minimize crime within their own neighborhoods.

The interesting contrast between the delinquency area and the urban village is summarized in Table 3.2.

Both organs of the convergent city are low in income, although the delinquency area is lower. The main differences, however, are in other features of the social structure. The urban village has a relatively more stable family structure, while the delinquency area has many families disrupted by divorce, widowhood, and various family problems, even within officially "intact" families. The population turnover is much lower in the urban village than in the delinquency area. Both organs reflect the ethnic diversity of the convergent city, but the urban village has stable dominance by one ethnic group, while the delinquency area reflects the

Table 3.2 Contrast Between Urban Village and Delinquency Area

Features	Urban Village	Deliquency Area
Income	lower middle	low to very low
Family structure	stable	unstable
Population turnover	low to moderate	very high
Ethnicity	stable	in flux
Rates of home ownership	at least moderate	very low
Streets	narrow, local, little traffic	busier streets
Scholarly coverage	Herbert Gans, Jane Jacobs	Shaw and McKay

invasion and succession of different groups in a shorter time span. Thus ethnicity in the delinquency area serves not as a means of social control but as a source of social disruption. In the urban village, even if homes are tiny, many are owner-occupied. This contrasts with very low levels of home ownership in delinquency areas, whose absentee landlords feel little responsibility for the local area. The urban village has small and narrow streets and little traffic. The delinquency area has at best mixed street patterns with some exposure to heavy traffic. Thus the urban village has many more stabilizing features than does the delinquency area.

We can describe the convergent city as a cluster of central districts, including the delinquency areas, that are surrounded by a patchwork of urban villages. The entire system is linked by its transportation corridors. We may think of the central districts and transportation corridors as the main crime producers, with the households and urban villages as the main organs of crime control. A double challenge faces these urban villages: first, they must minimize the amount of crime delivered to them by the transport system (offenders nip at their edges and then quickly escape into the transportation corridors); second, they must keep their own residents from getting into trouble when they leave the urban village for other destinations.

Overview of Crime's Progression

It would be nice to say that there is a simple linear progression, that the growth of crime is directly related to the growth of cities. But the reality is not so simple. At the first stage, the development of towns reduces rural crime by offering security from bandits. As towns develop into cities, local security begins to decline. The central districts and transportation corridors of the city provide anonymity to the offender, who can emerge from the crowd, commit a crime, and then lose himself in the crowd. The transportation corridors extend the range of potential offenders while exposing people to additional risks away from home (see Chapter 7). Yet the urban village, based on row houses, high fertility, pedestrian traffic, and women close to home, maintains a modicum of control.

The positive aspects of the convergent city are illustrated by describing some special parts of life today that remind us of the central districts and sidewalks of the convergent city of the past.

Today's Reminders
of the Convergent City

Modern society has at least three settings that produce the crowds of pedestrians common to the convergent city: the shopping mall, the college campus, and the nighttime entertainment district. All of these settings have dense pedestrian populations and a chance for people to watch one another. All three settings have high densities of strangers and high levels of crime.

Shopping Malls

In a shopping mall, many strangers converge, including many youths who "hang out." Even though most customers drive to the mall, its interior provides a sea of pedestrians that is reminiscent of the convergent city. A mall's multiplicity of shops and consumer goods not only provides much to buy but also much to look at for free. In short, a mall is more fun than today's suburban street.[12]

Drug sales and purchases are common in the central areas of some malls, where illegal buyers and sellers can easily find places to congregate or walk around. Contacts for illegal sales are readily concealed among the pedestrian flows. Stores have many goods suitable for shoplifting, and employees can steal even more. Substantial numbers of cars are parked where thefts of contents, accessories, and the cars themselves are not readily prevented. Cars carrying away illegally taken goods will have an undistinguished appearance. Personal attacks occur in parking lots and structures as people go in isolation to and from their cars.

College Campuses

What better place to find a pedestrian crowd than on a college campus? Students, staff members, and visitors are numerous and often unknown to one another. They converge at high density, often on foot and riding bicycles, with cars limited to the fringes of the campus. They are diverse in origins and interests. High-rise buildings are used for dormitories and offices. Virtually all parts of campus are accessible to all other parts, like the downtown of a convergent city. Crowds of people flow in and out of buildings, which contain many goods suitable for theft, including property belonging to the school, its employees, and its students. Bicycles are left outside where they are easy to steal and where the thief's illegal activity is camouflaged by the general flow of so many people.[13]

Students are at an age of high risk of victimization. Not only are some students offenders, but also nonstudent youths discover a sea in which they can swim unnoticed. Many students consume a good deal of alcohol, drawing some of them into crime as offenders or as victims. Some students are out late walking alone. Students with cars often have to park them in remote locations subject to risk of theft of car, contents, or accessories; they also may be subject to personal attack when traveling to and from their cars. The campus has many isolated nooks and crannies were students, staff members, and visitors alike are subject to illegal attack.

Thus the campus combines the old and the new: Like a convergent city of the past, it has crowds to watch; but like the metropolis of today, it has cars to steal.

Modern Entertainment Districts

Many metropolitan areas of today have entertainment districts that come alive at night or on weekends, reminding us of the convergent city of the past. An excellent example is the Westwood area near the University of California at Los Angeles (UCLA). Not only students, but also people from all around Los Angeles converge there by automobile for social purposes. Streets are blocked to limit automobile access to fringe areas; so people drive to the edge of the district, park their cars, then walk to restaurants, movies, or shops or simply cruise the area on foot.[14]

Densities on sidewalks and in stores and restaurants are far greater than the surrounding residential area or Los Angeles in general. Westwood has many crime problems, including shoplifting, fights, drunk and disorderly behavior, and even gang problems. Yet it continues to draw crowds of people who seem to enjoy looking at one another. They are willing to pay for parking and pay higher prices than for similar entertainment in less interesting parts of town. Perhaps Southern California's residents are sometimes bored with their usually quiet lives at low and moderate population densities.

What Is Missing?

We see that the shopping mall, college campus, and nighttime entertainment district offer modern reminders of the convergent city of the past. Yet something human is missing: People who are blind, obese, very thin, sickly, or with profound limps. The mall, the campus, and the entertainment district are for crowds of young people and those in vigorous middle age. At the campus and the entertainment district, children and older people do not belong. The shopping mall does best in replicating the convergent city of the past, because children and old people are there; but even at the mall, those who are less than healthy tend to stay away, while elderly people who cannot drive have a problem getting there. Because all three of these reminders of the convergent cities rely largely on automobiles for access by participants, they cannot replicate the convergent city of the past.

The Convergent City in Balance

We have lost something as the convergent city passes into oblivion in most of the United States. Perhaps its genuine benefits explain why so many North Americans love to visit or live in Manhattan, Boston, Toronto, Montreal, older parts of Chicago, and other places that have preserved much of the character of the convergent city.

Given its economic and social amenities, why did the convergent city give way to a new stage of everyday organization? Whatever our nostalgia for it, the convergent city produced congestion, noise, annoyance, and crime. Its high density ensured that you could hear ambulances and police sirens day and night and that other people's problems would impinge on you far more than you would like. A visit to Manhattan is all we need for a quick reminder that the convergent city is expensive, gets on one's nerves, and makes it hard to raise a family—without denying its tremendous opportunities in many realms of life.[15]

The twin search for affordable real estate and peace of mind help explain what followed.

Questions for Writing, Reflection, and Debate

---

1. Describe street life in a convergent city, based on some places you have seen and what you have read.

2. "In some stages of history, the greatest dangers are from outside your settlement. In other stages of history, the greatest danger is from within your settlement." Discuss this statement.

3. "Human history is a history of solving problems, then finding that the human solution produces a whole new set of problems." Apply this point to crime and security.

Sources for Ideas

This chapter is derived from basic urban theory and analysis. It stems in large part from my own undergraduate training at the University of Chicago, where I enrolled in an interdisciplinary course called "The Modern City." This course was taught by Harold Mayer and Gerhard Meyer and included many of the classic works on the city, its structure, history, ecology, and economics. The best single source of such information is Amos Hawley's *Urban Society: An Ecological Approach* (1971). Another source of the fundamentals guiding this chapter is Professor Hawley's classic work *Human Ecology: A Theory of Community Structure* (1950). That volume outlines the principles of human ecology as systematically as they have ever been put. The examples may be old, but the principles still hold today. Basic biological ideas such as symbiosis and commensalism are applied to human society. The spatial and temporal aspects of human activities are described. This book teaches us in clear and vigorous writing how to think systematically about community life.

These fundamentals are captured in a short but neat classic by Otis Dudley Duncan, "Human Ecology and Population Studies" (1959). Duncan summarizes and applies the concepts of human ecology neatly. His acronym POET stands for population, organization, environment, and technology. These four concepts help us think about social change, since a human population (P) adapts to its environment (E), using technology (T) and organization (O) to do so.

Endnotes

---

1. For links between urban structure and daily life, see Hawley (1971), as well as Gilmore (1953), Hawley (1950), McKenzie (1934), Mumford (1961), Park (1967), Simmel (1969), and Wirth (1964).

2. On rural banditry in the village and town stages, see Hobsbawm (1969). See also Barlow (1990), pages 216-220.

3. On the rookeries of London and other dangerous neighborhoods in early cities, see Brantingham and Brantingham (1984).

4. On both Manhattan and street traffic, see Whyte (1988). More citations on street traffic are offered in the notes for Chapter 8.

5. A social portrait of life in New York City is found in Glazer and Moynihan (1970).

6. Evidence that New York City combines the convergent city with a more modern metropolitan system is found by examining the American Automobile Association's 1990 map "New York City and Vicinity: Including Long Island."

7. Excellent remnants of convergent cities are found in the older sections of Toronto and Montreal, Canada. With their reliance on public transit, neighborhood ethnic homogeneity, tightly packed row houses, and stable residences, urban villages help Toronto and Montreal achieve very low urban crime rates when compared with other North American cities. In these cities it is fairly easy for people to watch their small homes, gardens, and the small piece of sidewalk and street in front of their houses. The row houses offer little space for burglars to enter, and the narrow streets become semiprivate space that is amenable to guardianship. This is exactly the point of Jane Jacobs's *Death and Life of Great American Cities* (1961). These two Canadian cities combine the pedestrian traffic produced by public transit with very cold weather, making it difficult for would-be offenders to linger on the street.

8. This section is distilled from basic urban research as reported in Hawley (1971). The central business district is the topic in both Rannals (1955) and Chapter 5 of Hawley (1971). For a more detailed examination of urban land uses by specific function, see Smith (1971). On CBD growth, see Bowden (1975).

9. Crime within transportation systems is reviewed in Easteal and Wilson (1991), LeVine and Wachs (1985), and Richards and Hoel (1980).

10. On security in the animal kingdom, see Ricklefs (1979).

11. For original work on the urban village, see Gans (1962). Also see Bollens and Schmandt (1970). Jacobs (1961), of course, deals extensively with the urban neighborhood.

12. For more on shopping malls, see Whyte (1988, pp. 203, 204, 206) and Kowinski (1985).

13. Campus crime is covered by tables in the *Uniform Crime Reports* and in equivalent reports at the state level. For example, see Illinois Law Enforcement Commission (1984).

14. On links between crime and entertainment areas, see Roncek and Maier (1991).

15. The annoyances of the urban environment are examined in Michelson (1976), especially Chapters 3 and 7. For other interesting and nerve-wracking aspects of city life, see Simmel (1969) and Wirth (1964).

4

The Divergent Metropolis:
More Crime Than Cities

The machine does not isolate man
from the great problems of nature
but plunges him more deeply into them.

—Antoine de Saint-Exupery
(Wind, Sand and Stars, 1939, p. 3; trans. by L. Galantiere)

The far right column of Table 3.1 shows the metro stage in the history of everyday life. This new chapter is about that stage and how it reduced social control even more than the era of the convergent city. Its dependence on automotive travel, its daily span of 50 miles, its large population—all of these make it a unique period in human history.

Important social forces helped to create the metro stage, but sometimes individuals also contribute to the forces of history.

Inventing the Modern Metropolis

Two individuals contributed inventions that helped to produce the modern metropolis and life as we now know it in the United States.

Inventing the Interstate Highway System

Soon after graduating from the U.S. Military Academy at West Point in 1915, young Dwight D. Eisenhower was appointed as temporary lieutenant colonel due to World War I. He was assigned to administrative work, and the war ended before he could go to Europe. Dejected by his nonparticipation in the war, Eisenhower joined an Army truck convoy in 1919 for a cross-continent journey that afforded him a chance to see the country. This convoy had no purpose other than to test Army equipment, display it to the public, and demonstrate the need for new roads. The convoy was slow and inefficient in its travel, a point that stuck in the 29-year-old officer's mind.[1]

Thirty-seven years later, as President of the United States, Eisenhower signed a bill that inaugurated the Interstate Highway System. The same system that allows us to drive coast to coast without a traffic light also helped to create the divergent metropolis by linking many local communities and making empty spaces near cities suitable for development. The Interstate Highway System made it easy for residential, business, and industrial areas to continue to leapfrog farther and farther from the city center. This highway system did much to alter the American social landscape, and a case can be made that Dwight Eisenhower is the president who did the most to invent the United States as we know it.

Inventing Suburban Mass Housing

Before World War II, William Levitt was a developer of expensive suburban housing. When the war came, he entered the U.S. Navy's construction battalion and learned to put up wartime buildings quickly. Discharged from the Navy after the war, Levitt learned that the housing shortage was chronic. He decided to do something about it, inventing a mass-produced suburb that he called Levittown. Starting on a potato field in Long Island, New York, Levitt organized the opposite of a moving assembly line: The work stayed on each home site, but specialized workers continued to move from one site to the next. His teams finished 35 houses a day at a single development. He sold most of these houses to veterans, no money down, for $65 a month. Levitt applied these methods in many other places, and his methods were copied throughout the nation.[2] The government inventions of low-interest loans to buy homes via the Veterans Administration and the Federal Housing Administration contributed to this spread of low-cost, single-family housing in suburban areas.

With housing and roads, the metropolis could and did develop. The following section summarizes the stages and terminology.

The Divergent Metropolis
and the Great Metropolitan Reef

Since World War II, the growth of the metropolis has been a continuous process (Table 4.1). The left side of the figure shows the five steps in the

Table 4.1 Growth of the Metropolis Since World War II

Changes	Terms
	A. Convergent city
1. Bedroom suburbs develop	
2. Shopping shifts to suburbs	
3. Workplaces shift to suburbs	B. Divergent metropolis
4. Area fills in between corridors	
5. Metropolises fuse	C. Great metropolitan reef

process, while the right-hand side presents the terminology. The first step is the development of bedroom suburbs. These are located on travel corridors into the central city and rely on trains or cars. Such suburbs are like towns and have low crime rates. This shift of shopping to suburban areas produces major declines in sales for downtown stores. Compared to the old downtown stores, the new suburban stores spread vast quantities of goods over a wide expanse of space with fewer employees to watch them. This invites people of all ages to shoplift. Parking lots for these stores assemble millions of dollars' worth of automobiles into a vast expanse of asphalt with virtually nobody to watch them.

If we examine suburbia during the 1950s, suburban crime problems were limited by three factors:

1. Most suburban youths did not yet have automobiles available to them, so their span of crime was not wide.

2. Suburban areas had not yet grown together, so stores were often far from residential areas, which were insulated by open spaces from one another.

3. Mothers are still outside the labor force and able to protect residential areas from crime.

With the dispersion of residences and shopping to suburbs, and increasing reliance on automobiles, employers begin to find that central city workplaces were inconvenient to their labor force. They purchased land at lower costs in outlying areas to construct factories, offices, and parking lots.

Suburbanization of work did not mean that people worked closer to home.[3] Jobs began to spread out over more suburban space, and not necessarily in the same places as residential suburbs. Large suburban plants could not possibly fill their labor force with local residents alone. With the automobile easily assembling a labor force, the average length of the trip to work continued to increase.

So homes, stores, and workplaces dispersed over increasing suburban spaces. The resulting *divergent metropolis* was characterized by movement outward from the center. At first, the divergent metropolis followed main road arteries and formed a patchwork of development. In time, the areas between the lines and patches filled in with additional development: residential, shopping, factory, and office. Growth continued outward and towns grew together.

In time, even metropolises themselves begin to fuse into a single organism, a seemingly endless suburban sprawl at moderate or low metropolitan density. In sum, the divergent metropolis becomes part of a great metropolitan reef. Each new piece of suburb fastens onto this "metroreef" like coral, building outward and connecting inward. The metroreef not only grows like coral but also functions like a coral reef after growth has taken place, with organisms moving about the reef continuously and diffusely. We do not abandon the term *divergent metropolis*, because some areas have not yet reached the metroreef stage.

Living systems have a fascinating way of proliferating until they transform themselves. This point is illustrated in the case of Los Angeles.[4]

The Growth of Los Angeles

Los Angeles did not actually spread out by the automobile alone but by a two-step process. First, long streetcar routes linked many towns in the Los Angeles area. Second, automotive travel allowed people to fill in the vast areas between the streetcar routes. Los Angeles grew like an amoeba ingesting food particles: reaching out, surrounding, and then absorbing each nearby town. More and more space was drawn into the metropolis, allowing people to live at low metropolitan densities and use automobiles to make up the distance. Government policy was to build roads, thus feeding this dispersal process. Not only did many small cities grow together, but also several independent cities did the same, including Pasadena, San Bernardino, Los Angeles, and Long Beach. Moreover, San Diego and Los Angeles grew somewhat together, blocked only by the large expanse of the Cleveland National Forest and Camp Pendleton, a U.S. Marine base.

We have described the stages leading from the bedroom suburb to the great metropolitan reef. We have presented Los Angeles as an example and discussed the developing crime opportunities. Now we detail how the divergent metropolis unpacked basic human activities.

Unpacking Human Activities

The new growth was at lower population densities for several reasons.

Dispersive Construction

Homes and other buildings were spreading over more metropolitan space. This occurred for five basic reasons:

1. Single family homes predominated.
2. Most homes were built with only one or two floors or stories.
3. Homes were placed on large lots.
4. Commercial and industrial buildings were built with only one or two stories on large lots.
5. A great deal of space was used for freeways,[5] boulevards, large parks, large schools (see Chapter 6), and vast parking lots. Much of this space became pure public space not readily subject to control (see Chapter 2).[6]

The divergent metropolis disperses property over so much space that it is very difficult for police to patrol effectively (see Chapter 1). When called to the scene of a crime, police have a great deal of distance to travel to get there, while the offenders have plenty of space in which to disappear and fewer witnesses around to recognize them. Police foot patrols become nearly impossible in divergent metropolises, and so they tend to lose the possibility of close contact with citizens and their property.[7] The distance among homes also makes it more difficult for neighbors to know when trouble is present and to assist one another.

Household burglary in the divergent metropolis tends to be more common than in convergent cities. Individual houses provide burglars access on all sides and offer significant privacy, with yards, fences, and shrubs helping to mask illegal entry.[8]

Dispersing People Across More Households

In the divergent metropolis, young couples and grandparents generally have their own households, while boarders are rarely found. Divorce rates are high, and divorcees usually move into their own households. College students tend to live away from home. All in all, we see a dispersion of people over increasing numbers of households.[9] This means that fewer people are home to provide guardianship against property crime or to protect one another from intruders and that activities away from home are less likely to occur in family groupings. As Chapter 2 indicated, when people are spread over more households, they have proportionally more property crime and violent crime victimizations both at home and elsewhere.

Dispersing Travelers Into More Vehicles

In the convergent city, many riders would fill public transit cars and buses. In the divergent metropolis, motorists are at risk when they stop to park or leave a building to go to their car. Parking lots and structures create extra crime risks for person and property; a vast number of largely unsupervised vehicles and their contents and accessories attract thieves and vandals. A row of cars can be used as a wall behind which offenders carry out other crimes unnoticed. Automobiles also can be used as weapons or as vehicles for offenders to travel to or from the scenes of other crimes. Inside cars, offenders can rape, attack, sell and consume illegal items, including drugs, and indulge in prostitution. When the divergent metropolis produces pedestrians, they travel to and from their cars, often walking alone; their trips on foot are episodic. This makes it easier for offenders to lay in wait and pick them off individually.[10]

On the other hand, the low density of the automobile-based metropolis makes it possible for more people to have personal garages beside or behind their single-family homes. This helps to reduce their risk of auto theft. The highest risk of auto theft is in cities with many cars but without convenient parking areas; automobile owners must park great distances away from work or shopping and cannot easily see their vehicles.

As significant as automobiles themselves is the change in routine activities they produce. By taking pedestrians off the street, they vastly increase the ability of offenders to find victims free from guardians. This allows illegal sales and consumption to move into public areas, while also feeding predatory crimes. Automobiles in the divergent metropolis draw riders away from public transit, leaving its cars and stations highly vulnerable to crime. On the other hand, the pickpocketing that goes with crowded public transit in the convergent city declines as the divergent metropolis takes over.

Dispersing Activities Away From Families and Households

In the convergent city, activities tended to be localized and people tended to be home relatively often. Dense neighborhoods of people who had no cars produced natural conversations over the backyard fence or on the porch or street. Today's divergent metropolis not only disperses people and households, but also helps people to avoid interaction with neighbors while it increases face-to-face interaction with people who live several miles away. Indeed, friends and merchants far from home can be reached by simply entering a car and stepping on the gas pedal. Thus activities have tended to disperse from household and neighborhood. Evidence of the dispersion of activities away from the household is the major increase in the number of households empty when Census Bureau personnel and other survey researchers call. A dispersion away from neighborhood activities is evidenced by the decline of small grocery stores and the rise of ever-larger supermarkets and other stores. More to the point, most of the customers for stores get there by car, not by foot. The multicar family and females holding drivers' licenses freed them from household and neighborhood confinement. For both males and females, automobiles widened the spatial span for selecting human contacts, allowing people to ignore those who were spatially closest and find others with whom to interact.

Perhaps the most important element in dispersing activities away from the household was the entry of married women into the labor force. This entry served to depopulate the residential area during weekdays. Boys and girls of school ages are away until approximately 3 p.m. Younger children are increasingly sent to preschools. The elderly may remain in a neighborhood, but they are too thinly dispersed to be very effective in counteracting crime.

Summary

We have shown that the divergent metropolis serves to unpack human activities. It disperses people over more households, households and construction over more metropolitan space, travelers over more vehicles, and activities away from household and family settings.

Table 4.2 summarizes the consequences of these dispersions and social control within the settlement itself. In the village and town stages, local social control is strong. In the convergent city, these dimensions differ by location. Within central districts and transportation corridors, local social control is weak, while this same control can be strong within urban villages. In contrast, the divergent metropolis weakens localism,[11] with the loss of control producing even higher levels of crime.[12]

Table 4.2 Social Control and Urban Growth

Stage in the History of Everyday Life	Local Social Control
Village	high
Town	high
Convergent city	
Central districts and transportation corridors	low to medium
Urban village	medium to high
Divergent metropolis	low

The vast increment in purely public space within the divergent metropolis plays a major role in undermining the capacity of local people to control their environment and prevent crime. This helps us to explain why crime rates are so high in the United States.

Questions for Writing, Reflection, and Debate

1. Get maps of Los Angeles and five old convergent cities of Europe (for example, Paris, Amsterdam, Brussels, Copenhagen, and Stockholm). Bring the cities to the same scale and overlay the old cities onto the Los Angeles map. Then find out how much population all six cities have in how much space.

2. Several "divergent" aspects of the modern metropolis are discussed. Which do you think are most important for changing crime rates? Defend your answer.

3. How do mass transit systems serve to produce and prevent crime?

˙ Sources for Ideas

One of the best ways to understand the development of the divergent metropolis is to read about how it happened in a city you know. Two volumes by geographers come to mind. Those who have a feel for Chicago should see Berry, Cutler, Draine, Kiang, Tocalis, and de Vise (1976). Two chapter titles—"The Suburban Frontier" and "The Metabolism of a Metropolis"—give a flavor of what that text offers. Those who are more interested in Los Angeles should see Nelson and Clark (1976). This book pays attention to population density and physical movement in the course of a day. A more recent and very useful reference on greater Los Angeles is Heer and Herman (1990).

For those who are interested in changes in American families and households, various works by Paul Glick are extremely helpful. For example, see Glick (1984). Another source applying to a longer period of time is Seward (1978). For a more recent and detailed study of family and household, see Sweet and Bumpass (1987), a careful description of American households based on the 1980 U.S. census. Pay special attention to Chapter 9 on households.

For a study of crime trends in suburbs, see an article by Stahura and Huff (1986), which shows the increases in crime from census year to census year by distance from the center. The suburbs suffer more increase proportionally than the central cities, contrary to what you might guess from the news coverage. However, major crime growth is dramatic throughout the metropolitan areas during this period.

Endnotes

1. On Eisenhower and his cross-country trip, see Ambrose (1984), pages 65-69.

2. The story of William Levitt was drawn from *Consumer Reports* (1980).

3. Suburbanization of industry is taken up by Kitagawa and Bogue (1955).

4. For a thorough description of Los Angeles as an urban system, see Nelson and Clark (1976).

5. Information on freeways was drawn from the Automobile Club of Southern California's 1988 map of the Los Angeles area.

6. During the 1950s, high-rise public housing actually reduced the population density of the low-level neighborhoods they replaced (Jacobs, 1961). This surprising outcome occurred for two reasons: (a) much of the inside space was lost to stairwells and hallways, and (b) much of the outside space was left open. These public spaces were subject to low levels of social control and quickly fed the crime problem in public housing complexes. On the unpacking of the city and for an overview of metropolitanization, see Hawley (1956). Also see Gottman (1961) and Hoover and Vernon (1959). For more on urban metropolitan change, see Berry, Cutler, Draine, Kiang, Tocalis, and de Vise (1976).

7. Patrol problems are exemplified by the Kansas City Patrol Experiment, which was cited in Chapter 1.

8. Household burglary is detailed in Cromwell, Olson, and Avary (1991) and Bennett and Wright (1984).

9. On dispersing people over more households and households over more space, see Glick (1984). Household and family changes are further described in Seward (1978) and Sweet and Bumpass (1987), which is a careful description of U.S. households based on the 1980 census.

10. People over more vehicles brings with it automobile-related crimes; see Clarke and Harris (1992). On transit crime in a divergent metropolis, note LeVine and Wachs (1985) and Richards and Hoel (1980).

11. Many words denoting localism are still used in American life today. These words have different meanings than they did in the past and should not mislead us when we evaluate city life today. These terms can give an illusion of the past without the real thing. First, many areas of cities still call themselves "neighborhoods" and use their old names. However, when few people walk to the store and carry back their groceries in a cart, this is not the old concept of neighborhood. When corner bars and friends visited on foot give way to those visited by car, they are no longer local in the sense of the convergent city. Without routine pedestrian traffic and a daytime population of local adults, the word *neighborhood* takes on a new meaning. Second, ethnic areas remain in large cities, but they generally have a different character than in the convergent city of the past (see Nelson & Clark, 1976). Thus the Chinese population of Los Angeles is dispersed around the metropolis, even if many

Chinese Americans drive their cars back to Chinatown for weekend shopping. Similarly, old Jewish neighborhoods still have some Jewish institutions (see Gans, 1962), but they depend on adequate parking because Jewish customers arrive mainly by car from other areas. Third, mass transit systems continue to exist and even to be constructed (in Los Angeles), and yet they continue to lose out to automotive travel. Even in the old Eastern cities, auto trips are dominant outside the central district.

12. As noted in Table 4.1, the low level of social control for the divergent metropolis is evidenced by growing suburban crime rates. Note Stahura and Huff (1986).

5

Adolescence, Home Life, and Social Control

Drive Nature from your door with a pitchfork,
and she will return again and again.

—Horace (Epistles, 1.10)

We are the slaves of objects around us,
and appear little or important according
as these contract or give us room to expand.

—Goethe (in J. P. Eckermann, Conversations with Goethe, 11 September 1828)

This chapter is about changes in adolescence and in the structure of home life.[1] We discuss how the function of the teenager in society has changed to produce a mismatch between teenagers' natural abilities and the tasks available for them to do. This mismatch not only leaves teenagers without a satisfactory position in society, but also undermines informal social control. Control has also been reduced by certain products that are available in our society, while jobs for adolescents have not necessarily served to compensate for the losses of control. The conclusion is that modern society puts adolescents in a position of greater participation in crime. To explain these varied changes, we need first to examine adolescence in general.

General Adolescent Characteristics

The literature on growth traits of adolescents shows that the onset of puberty brings these characteristics:

* increases in stamina, acuity, and activity levels;

* acceleration of physical growth;

* development of reproductive capacities;

- acceleration of muscular growth (in males); and
- interest in sex.

Adolescents are full of energy; they have trouble sitting still and need something to do. They become sexually attractive, are ready to reproduce, and have the energy to raise their own families.[2] Indeed, they are physically prepared for two traditional and serious human tasks: doing work and raising a family.[3]

The next part of this chapter, for comparison purposes, draws from an interesting literary source to describe basic work and family tasks that were common before this century.

The Foxfire Era:
A Glimpse of the Past

Sometimes important information from the past is found fossilized somewhere in the present. In the Appalachian mountain region of the eastern United States, for example, many villages and farms have been so isolated that they preserved well into this century many patterns of life from the nineteenth century. These patterns were collected in great detail by Eliot Wigginton for *Foxfire* magazine and six *Foxfire* books published from 1972 to 1980.

These books chronicle in detail how work was done in a many areas of early America. Every activity is described in the old-fashioned way. For example, "how-to" diagrams show how to make hampers, baskets, brooms, brushes, mops, and chairs; fiddles, banjos, and dulcimers; wagon wheels, wagons, yokes, and a foot-powered lathe; knives, guns, butter churns, tar, cheese, soap, and apple butter. Other activities include raising cattle, sheep, and hogs; smoking meat and tanning hides; iron making and blacksmithing; bear hunting; logging and wood carving; corn shucking; washing clothes in an iron pot; cooking on a fireplace and wood stove or in a dutch oven. None of these tasks are performed with electricity or other modern conveniences.[4]

Two main points come to mind from the Foxfire books. First, most of these traditional tasks placed great physical demands on people. Physical strength and endurance were necessary to work in the Foxfire world, more so than in the world as we know it today.

Second, as meticulous as the Foxfire books are and despite their great effort to record and pass on dying traditions, a reader would have trouble performing these tasks from the book alone. How much pressure do you apply when tanning a hide? How loud do you yell at a hog to get its attention? How tight do you tie the cornhusks to make an old-style broom? Experience can teach you slowly the answers to these questions, but the best way to learn them is to watch other people who know what they are doing. The main reason the Foxfire books were written and read was that so few people were around who could demonstrate how to make a wagon wheel. But the Foxfire books were not necessary when members of the older generation were around to pass these skills on to the next generation as a matter of course.

Adolescents and Home Life in the Foxfire Era

We will now put together what we learned in the previous section on general adolescent characteristics with the current section on the Foxfire era.[5]

Productive Roles

In the realm of everyday work, the Foxfire world was well suited to adolescents. Their physical stamina and strength, acuity of senses, and ability to watch and learn how to perform tasks would serve them well in everyday tasks of the sorts described earlier. And by these tasks they could burn their burgeoning energy. This gave them an important economic function.

Reproductive Roles

Teenagers' important economic function also gave them a legitimate reproductive function. Suitable as workers, teenagers were also ripe for marriage and child rearing.[6] During the nineteenth century, these characteristics were common in the United States:

- ◆ Females would typically marry at age 16 or 17 or even younger.
- ◆ Males would typically marry at 18 or 19 or younger.

- Babies would start to arrive soon thereafter.
- Males would already be in the labor force, whether as farmers or in some other occupation.
- Schooling would already have been completed.

In short, adult roles were well under way. Table 5.1 shows the main stages in a girl's reproductive life.

Table 5.1 Main Stages in a Girl's Reproductive Life

Girl's Age	Event
14	onset of puberty
15	truly ready to become pregnant
16	ready to give birth and to marry

Consider that the period from 14 to 15 is a time of postmenarchal subfecundity, during which a girl has low risk of pregnancy because her systems are not quite developed. Thus a girl exposed to sexual intercourse right after puberty probably is not pregnant until age 15 and is not ready to give birth until age 16, by which time she is married anyway. Those girls who were having intercourse would be inclined to marry quickly so as not to get "caught" by pregnancy; but if that happened, a wedding date could be moved up to legitimate a pregnancy.

Timing of Life's Transitions in the Foxfire Era

Thus the Foxfire society had these four phenomena timed about right:

1. the end of schooling
2. sexual maturation
3. sexual union
4. major work responsibility

By the time one's sexual urges had ripened, society was ready to put them to use. By the time bodies had grown stronger, society was ready to put them to work.

The work structure of the Foxfire era would naturally bring together people of both sexes and different ages. Because youths were valuable in production, the older generation needed them around. Because youths were starting their own families, they were soon tied down by raising children and not readily available for crime and delinquency. Because sexual behavior could start legitimately at a young enough age, there was no need to worry about it as delinquent behavior.

Products and Home Life

The Foxfire era not only provided a role for youths, but also kept families generally close to home because of the basic demands of everyday life. The traditional cooking fuel was wood. A wood stove took quite a while to warm up and had to be tended and fed. This created necessary chores for family members, including parents and children, and helped tie them close to home and thus to one another. Foods could be preserved by smoking, salting, drying, and home canning, all performed in a family setting and again providing a technical and economic basis for family life. These methods did not preserve foods for as long a period as do modern preservatives, and fresh foods were available only according to local seasons. Quick food outside the home was accessible in berry and apple seasons, but not in general.

When a meal was cooked, leftovers would not last long. Although a springhouse provided natural refrigeration from cold water, it could not compete with a modern freezer. Food could be frozen in winter outside, but it was subject to raids by wild animals. Thus the tenuous food supply of the Foxfire world kept families quite busy and together, spanning ages and sexes in symbiotic pursuit of survival.

The tedious washing of clothes in traditional washtubs had similar consequences for close family life. Such patterns of interaction made it difficult for youths to stray far from family settings.

Summing what this chapter has stated so far, the work roles, reproductive roles, and home life of the Foxfire era provided natural controls for young people, keeping them busy while offering a truly important place in society.

Since the Foxfire era, important changes have occurred in the role of teenagers. One of these is a biosocial change, which we will discuss in the following section.

Secular Trend
in the Timing of Puberty

Biologists have reported a secular trend toward younger ages of puberty. Their evidence strongly suggests that the age of puberty is partly determined by a protein-rich diet. Thus famines, by interfering with nutrition, serve to delay the onset of puberty for males and females. Less developed countries today, because of poor nutrition, have older ages of puberty. Developed countries today can look back in their history to an earlier era when nutrition levels were lower and the age of puberty older. When nutrition is poor, puberty typically occurs at age 14; when nutrition is rich, puberty occurs around age 12. These averages do not tell the story for every individual, but they provide an idea of what to expect for the population as a whole. However, this change in teenage roles goes beyond pubertal change and involves both productive and reproductive roles.

Adolescent Roles
in the Modern United States

In this section, we shall examine how modern society delivers temptations while removing controls, thus producing more crime. We begin by comparing modern productive roles in comparison to those of the Foxfire era.

Productive Roles

Much of our story is told in Table 5.2.

The following generalizations apply to this distribution of jobs in the United States today when compared with the Foxfire era's tasks.

◆　Most jobs today require several years of schooling. High school diplomas and higher education are common prerequisites.

◆　Few current jobs require substantial amounts of muscular strength or physical endurance.

◆　Substantial numbers of current jobs involve skills in working with people and data rather than skills in working with one's hands (dealing with "things").

Table 5.2 The Distribution of Occupations in the United States, 1991

Civilian Occupations	Employed (%)
Technical, sales, and administrative support	31
Managerial and professional specialty	23
Service	14
Precision production, craft, and repair	12
Machine operators and inspectors	6
Transportation and material moving	4
Farming, forestry, and fishing	4
Fabricators, assemblers, hand-working positions, handlers, equipment cleaners, helpers, and laborers	6
Total	100%

Sources: The percentage distribution of occupations is calculated from the 1992 *Statistical Abstract of the United States*, Table 629.

◆ Specialization is the order of the day. For example, the traditional occupation of "butcher" now includes animal stunner, shackler, sticker, head trimmer, carcass splitter, offal separator, shrouder, hide trimmer, boner, grader, smoked meat preparer, and hide handler.[7]

These four points have important implications for teenagers. Most current jobs make little use of their distinct advantages in muscular strength, physical endurance, and sensual acuity. Modern jobs instead put a premium on learning by experience how to deal with people or learning in class how to deal with data.

We can see how the characteristics of today's jobs conflict with the developing abilities of teenagers. These abilities fit better with the Foxfire tasks listed earlier. Herein lies the basic problem for teenagers in society today: They lack a suitable economic function. Instead, they must live for the future, preparing themselves in school in hopes that someday they will be economically useful to society.

Reproduction and the
Timing of Role Transitions

In stark contrast to the onset of adult roles in the Foxfire era, modern American youths typically follow this pattern:

- Youths remain in school through the teenage years and beyond.
- Youths marry during their 20s, typically after college.
- Youths work only part-time or part-year until their 20s.
- Sexual behavior begins in the midteen years and is often concealed from parents and with the intent of avoiding pregnancies.
- Intended fertility is delayed into the 20s.
- Many unintended pregnancies nonetheless occur and often end in abortion.
- During the teenage years, unintended pregnancies that are taken to term generally are not followed by marriage.

In short, the story of adolescence in the modern United States is a story of delayed adult roles in both work and reproduction. The most natural abilities of youths—to expend their energies in productive work and to raise families—do not fit the requirements of a modern labor force or the preparation time needed to enter it.

Modern timing is more like that shown in Table 5.3. With puberty beginning at 12, true readiness for pregnancy at 13, and marriage at 22 or older, almost a decade of risk of pregnancy is present before society is ready for a woman to take on adult roles. For males, the gap between onset of sexual capacity and commencement of family roles is as long or longer.[8]

Table 5.3 Modern Reproductive Timing

Girl's Age	Event
12	onset of puberty
13	truly ready to become pregnant
14	ready to give birth
15	
16	
17	
18	
19	
20	
21	
22	ready to marry

The same increase in protein that accelerates sexual maturation for youths also makes them bigger and stronger, thus physically even more ready for a world that no longer exists.

Puberty at an earlier age, stronger bodies, and the lack of adult reproductive and work roles together place youths out of sync with their own society. Yet they remain in tune with one another, ready for sexual intercourse whether their parents like it or not. They also are well suited to crime. Muscularity is highly useful for predatory crimes, fights, and for protecting other illegal behavior. Acuity of senses helps offenders avoid detection and counteraction by others. The physical endurance of youths helps them drink more and burn the candle at both ends. The sexual prowess of youth in the absence of a legitimate outlet leads to delinquency virtually by definition. The lack of adult roles allows adolescents to go off into a world of their own. Adult society, not valuing adolescent strengths, turns them over to one another. This change is reflected in several consumer products.

Modern Products and Home Life in the Divergent Metropolis

Many of the products of modern society are consistent with a dispersion of activities away from household and family settings.[9] As people are freed from household chores and other activities, adolescents are better able to evade controls.

Everyday Food

In modern society, much food production has shifted to factory settings. Households go to supermarkets to purchase prepared foods.[10] At home these foods require little or no cooking. When food is cooked, this is accomplished in little time on appliances that need little warming up and virtually no tending. Many such appliances have built-in timers that turn them on and off without a human presence even required. These appliances permit people to arrive home, eat quickly, and go out for the evening. Adolescents gain largely independent access to food, thus increasing their independence from the home and its controls. The wide availability of fast food prepared and served outside the home removes the need to return home for food at all. The improved preservatives, freezing, dependable refrigeration, and use of plastic wrapping and plastic containers also contribute to the ability of individuals to leave household settings for most of the day and night and still be able to eat. Frozen foods minimize preparation, thus speeding the meal and cutting cleanup time. Any child old enough to place a frozen dinner in a microwave oven is old enough to avoid family meals. No pots, pans, peelers, graters, mixing bowls, or blenders need be dirtied. The frozen pan is discarded, and a youth can go off with peers. This loss of maternal control over the means of refreshment is part and parcel of reduced control. No longer needing maternal assistance for refueling, youths have less need to check in at home and can answer parental questions later, after they have had some time to think of the answers.

Large Containers, Stores, and Refrigerators

From store to garbage can, we can list the seven steps of consumption in the divergent metropolis:

1. Drive car once a week to large grocery store;
2. fill large grocery cart with large containers;
3. pack large containers into large grocery bags;
4. take bags to car, pack car, drive home, unload car;
5. load groceries into large refrigerator and large cupboards;
6. eat and drink large amounts; and
7. load large amounts of garbage into cans.

This pattern of activity depends on technology: automobiles to shop in, strong packaging, refrigeration, and preservatives. It involves once-a-week trips by car to stores a few miles away as opposed to daily walks to stores one or two blocks away. This in turn helps detach people from their own neighborhood, thus reducing informal control, while creating large self-service stores where shoplifting is easier and theft also tempts employees.

Frozen Bagels

Modern marketing makes it convenient to maintain an ethnic identity without an ethnic neighborhood. Frozen bagels, pizza, egg rolls, sukiyaki, moussaka, enchiladas, sauerbraten, and pirogi can all be purchased in large supermarkets. This undermines the traditional ethnic stores in local neighborhoods. It is not necessary to live in the original neighborhood or shop in the original store very often. Except for black-white segregation, residential areas become ethnically diverse, and homogeneous neighborhoods no longer provide extra social control in local areas.

Big Bottles of Whiskey

Alcohol distribution and liquor tax collection data show a dispersion of whiskey and beer consumption away from bars and toward package sales, plus a major increase in the share of whiskey that is sold in large bottles (e.g. gallon and half-gallon). As parents overstock their liquor cabinets with large bottles, their children can readily siphon off alcohol without drawing parental attention. Who will notice an inch missing from a very large bottle? Who would notice a bit of watering down? Package sales also make it easy for those who are barely old enough to buy liquor for their underage friends. Canned beer sold in packs of 24 also make it easy for beer to slip away from parental controls. Who needs to worry about parental supervision when one can easily consume alcohol in cars, parking lots, and lovers' lanes?

Everyday Washing

Modern washing machines and automatic dishwashers allow basic household chores to be carried out quickly and easily, often using built-in timers to further reduce the need of a resident to be at home. By ending the task of hanging wash on lines and removing it, automatic dryers render neighbors less likely to see one another or to watch their backyards, from which burglars often enter homes. Dishwashers and self-cleaning appliances make it easier to get away soon after dinner, allowing adolescents to escape chores and parental supervision of any sort. They also help different members of a family to cook what they want when they want it, without resorting to family dinners and other communal events that provide mutual guardianship and informal influence.

Transistors, Plastics, and Aluminum

Radios, televisions, and other electronic products were once very heavy and expensive instruments that had to be shared in family settings. For example, a 1950 television set was far too heavy to be easily stolen.

Transistors changed this, making small electronic goods possible. Plastics and aluminum also made continued development of light and inexpensive electronic goods possible. Thus each child could have a personal lightweight source of music for private listening. This allows much greater adolescent control over the airwaves and many more stealable consumer goods that can now be stolen from a thousand locations.

Air Conditioners

Before the advent of the air conditioner, a hot summer made life indoors almost unbearable. People sat on porches to stay cool and in doing so they discouraged burglars and other offenders by monitoring the whole street. The air conditioner makes indoors the preferred hot weather location, leaving the street unwatched and reducing contacts among neighbors. If many people are away from their neighborhoods and those who are there do not interact with the street, then who is left to take responsibility for it?

Telephones

On the one hand, adolescents can use the phone to arrange peer activities and evade parental controls. They also allow youths to call home, giving parents an illusion of control. Telephones can be used by burglars to check if residents are home and by obscene phone callers or others committing crimes of harassment.

Summary Thus Far

We have covered a good deal of ground. We began by offering a glimpse of the past via the Foxfire description of work in a bygone era. We proceeded to review the characteristics of adolescence and then to examine how the Foxfire era provided significant work and reproductive roles for adolescents, while keeping everyday work close to home.

Switching to today's society, we contrasted modern work and reproduction with the Foxfire era, demonstrating the much reduced role of adolescents. A fundamental disruption of timing for basic social roles renders them more likely to be involved in crime and delinquency, while the structure of everyday products is also consistent with a weaker home life and lower levels of control.

Modern society sometimes tries to compensate for these changes by providing part-time or part-year jobs for youths. The next section analyzes such opportunities, taking into account what we have learned about both the Foxfire era and modern times.

Compensatory Jobs for Youths: Bringing Back the Past?

The idleness insight from Chapter 1 states that idleness provides time for involvement in crime. This implies that work reduces the time for crime. Thus we can expect that jobs for youths will keep them away from criminal activity. This chapter would seem to reinforce that relationship, because the Foxfire era busied youth with work and kept them away from delinquency.

On the other hand, researchers have disappointed us by finding that high school students who have jobs also get involved in more rather than less crime (Ruggiero, Greenberger, & Steinberg, 1982; Greenberger & Steinberg, 1986; Gottfredson, 1985). That finding appears to conflict with basic control theory:

Work keeps youth busy in conventional activities.

They are too busy to commit criminal acts.

Therefore work prevents crime.

The finding is also extremely difficult to swallow from the responsibility standpoint:

Work provides youth with responsibility.

Responsibility makes a young person grow up.

Growing up makes a young person shy away from crime.

Hence work prevents youth from committing crime.

Why does such logic seem to hold for the Foxfire era, but not for today? To examine that question, we can list the characteristics of work for youths in the Foxfire era and today (see Table 5.4). In the Foxfire era, prosperity levels were low and work requirements heavy, both in time and physical demands. A 16-year-old would be working for survival of self and family.

Table 5.4 Work Circumstances for Youths in the Foxfire and Modern Eras

Circumstance	Foxfire Era	Modern Era
Prosperity level	low	high
Work period	full-time	part-time
Marital status	married or marriage imminent	single
Money used for	basic support of self, family	personal recreation
Physical demands	heavy and constant	limited
Job interaction with	family, other age groups	own age group
Crime opportunity at work	none	substantial

He or she would already be married or marriage would be imminent. When work was over, there was sleep. Work would occur within the family setting, not among young peers. In addition there would be virtually nothing to steal in the course of daily work.

The modern era, however, provides much higher levels of prosperity. The typical 16-year-old who works is not doing so to support self or family on a day-to-day basis, and he or she is not married or soon to be married. Earnings will go for recreation and extras, including gasoline money or car payments to help evade parental controls. The work itself places limited physical demands and leaves youths full of energy after finishing their jobs. The low-wage and low-skill jobs available to youths often are performed near other youths and with few adult workers around. Many jobs bring the worker closer to money and goods suitable for theft.

When a youth today finds a job, its function for society or self is very different than in the Foxfire past. We can see that the roles of adolescents have changed so fundamentally that sincere efforts to provide useful activities can easily backfire. This poses a difficult challenge to discover ways in which youths can find more suitable roles in modern society.

Summary

This chapter has described the roles of teenagers and family patterns for the modern era in contrast to the Foxfire era. That represents a period in which work was carried out without the use of modern energy sources. It includes both the village and town eras described in Chapter 3. But it also tells us something about the convergent city in the age of steam power. Even if nonhuman energy was available, a good deal of muscle was still needed to fuel and control machinery. Thus the role of adolescents continued to be secure until this century, when educational demands began to accelerate and the onset of work and marriage was pushed to later ages.

Do not read this chapter as a statement of nostalgia for the Foxfire era. Although crime opportunities may have been limited, it was an era of a much lower standard of living, high infant mortality, and limited opportunity. Like each of the eras we have discussed, it had its advantages and disadvantages. Few of us would turn the clock back to do our work with the difficult and inefficient methods of the past. However, we can see that these methods had some good consequences by providing natural controls that helped keep crime from getting out of hand.

Questions for Writing, Reflection, and Debate

---

1. Is there any way for society to change the role of adolescents or is it built into the fundamental structure of our economy?

2. Some people say that U.S. society places a premium on youth. Try to reconcile that statement with this chapter.

3. "The increased rates of premarital pregnancy are evidence of a decline in moral standards." Is this statement consistent with or in conflict with the points made in this chapter?

4. Discuss some inventions and products not mentioned in this chapter that (a) serve to increase crime and (b) serve to reduce crime.

Sources for Ideas

For more information on the changing concept of adolescence, its origin and historical development, see Kett (1977). Kett reminds us that both the term and the concept of *adolescence* are relatively new in history. That author puts adolescence into historical perspective, but I wonder whether he exaggerates how badly children were treated in the past.

A wonderful source of details about thousands of real jobs in modern society is the *Dictionary of Occupational Titles* (DOT) published by the U.S. Department of Labor (1991). Each job is described in words; its duties requirements are stated, including dealing with people, data, and things; physical demands and strength; and educational and vocational preparation.

Several sources provide us with insights about how everyday tasks and products change over time. A famous source is Braudel (1979). Another excellent source of information on everyday life is Petroski (1993); also see Petroski (1992) for the history of a single useful object through the ages— the pencil. A modern reprint is available for the 1902 Sears and Roebuck catalog (New York: Crown Books, 1969). This illustrated, black-and-white volume teaches us a lot about what daily life was like then and how different it was from modern life. See especially household goods shown on pages 560-602 and 721-740, noting the physical dimensions of these and other items. Several other Sears catalogs are available in libraries, showing how products have changed over the past 50 years. For information on modern products and their impact on history, see *Consumer Reports* (1980). My favorite essays in that book are those on shopping malls, suburbia, transparent tape, latex paint, washers and dryers, disposable diapers, compact discs, and videocassette recorders.

Many of the ideas of this chapter derive from the work of William F. Ogburn on the role of inventions in social change and on the changing functions of the family. The easiest way to introduce yourself to his ideas is through *On Culture and Social Change: Selected Papers* (1964); see especially Papers 5 and 14. For a general theory of inventions as they relate to the larger society, see Gilfillan (1935). Among the questions Gilfillan asks is, "Who invented the ship?"

Endnotes

1. On adolescent characteristics and the transition to adolescence, see Montemayor, Adams, and Gullotta (1990). Also see Coleman (1980). Concerning physical growth and changing performance, see Malina (1990) (note the bibliography). See also Simmons and Blyth (1987). On changes in physical performance, see Beunen and Malina (1988) and Carron and Bailey (1974).

2. On the historical change in the productive and reproductive roles of adolescence in society, see Kett (1977).

3. On marital and family patterns from the past, see Seward (1978).

4. The information on products, home life, and tasks in the Foxfire era was extracted from the *Foxfire* books, whose tables of contents refer precisely to the tasks described. See Wigginton (1972, 1973, 1975, 1977, 1979, 1980).

5. We treat the "Foxfire era" as a rough equivalent of the premodern era, including village and town stages of history. However, the era of the convergent city has some elements of the Foxfire era, because machinery was heavy and hard to control, requiring muscle and providing roles for adolescents. Thus the basic points made in this chapter contrast the era of the divergent metropolis with the entire period before it arose.

6. On the trend toward earlier puberty, see references in Tanner (1962).

7. The last two points are drawn from the 1991 edition of the *Dictionary of Occupational Titles*.

8. On marital and family patterns and trends in recent years, see Glick (1984) and Sweet and Bumpass (1987).

9. Sources on modern products include Petroski (1993), Panati (1987), and *Consumer Reports* (1980). For a longer-term perspective, consult Braudel (1979).

10. For comparisons of trends in purchases from eating places versus food stores, see the 1989 *Statistical Abstract of the United States*, Table 1329 and following tables; see Table 1325 to compare grocery store sales; see Tables 1329 and 1334 for relative sales by liquor stores, bars, and taverns. On whiskey and beer sales, see annual reports of the U.S. Bureau of Alcohol, Tobacco, and Firearms. As indicators of container usage, see the 1990 *Statistical Abstract of the United States*, Table 350 (solid-waste generation trends). On washing machines and dryers, see *Consumer Reports* (1980). On sales of lightweight durables, electronic appliances, and other appliances, see the 1989 *Statistical Abstract of the United States*, Tables 1305 through 1321. On the changing use of telephones and other communications, see Pool (1977).

6

Large Schools for Adolescents

This country was built by people educated in a
one-room schoolhouse by the farmer's daughter,
who was educated in that same schoolhouse.

—*C. Arnold Anderson*
(from a 1969 lecture at the University of Chicago)

We shape our buildings;
thereafter they shape us.

—*Sir Winston Churchill*
(Time, *September 12, 1960*)

This chapter compares the schools of the convergent city to those of the divergent metropolis. We emphasize control factors that serve to prevent crime in school settings. We are concerned not only about crime that occurs inside a building but also about crime that occurs on school grounds or very close to them. We are concerned not only with crime that occurs during school hours but also with crime that occurs during lunch breaks or after school. Our argument in this chapter is that the large schools of the divergent metropolis interfere with informal social control and produce more crime.[1] In the next section we compare the small school of the convergent city to the large school of the divergent metropolis.

School Size and Setting

Table 6.1 compares the schools of the urban past to those of the metropolitan present along a dozen different dimensions. The table's first and most prominent feature of comparison is that schools in the convergent city are much smaller than those of the divergent metropolis.

For example, an elementary school during the era of the convergent metropolis enrolled some 300 pupils; the modern period enrolls some 900. A secondary school enrolled approximately 600 as compared to 2,000 or

Table 6.1 Schools of the Convergent City Compared With Those of the Divergent Metropolis

Characteristics	Schools	
	Convergent City	Divergent Metropolis
Number of students		
Elementary:	300	900
Secondary:	600	2,000 to 3,000
Grade splits	elementary (1-8)	elementary (1-6)
		middle (7-8)*
	secondary (9-12)	high (9-12)
Stories or floors	3 or 4	1 or 2
Hallways and stairwells	few	many
Grounds	small	large
Teachers per acre	many	few
Landscaping	minimal	substantial
Teachers recognize most students	yes	no
Worst 1% of students (no.)	3 to 6	20 to 30
Activity participation rates	high	low
Curricular variety	low	high

*Gradespans vary from place to place.

more in the divergent metropolis. In short, we see a three- to fourfold increase in the number of students per school. This increase in size occurs despite the modern tendency to split schooling into three phases, with a middle school sandwiched between elementary school and high school.

Another important aspect of comparison is the physical building and grounds. Schools in the convergent metropolis are compact in space, using a single building of three or four stories. The school building is situated on a small cement lot, providing limited area for student recreation and little or no greenery.

In contrast, the large school of the divergent metropolis not only requires more inside space for size alone, but also uses only one or two stories. Thus the divergent metropolis school buildings spread over a larger area, often having a campus including several buildings, generally with extra acreage and landscaping. Even though the modern school has many more teachers, it has far fewer teachers per acre than the compact school of the convergent city. These structural differences between the schools of the convergent city and the divergent metropolis are very relevant to social control in general and crime in specific. We begin by discussing control based on numbers alone.[2]

Control Factors
Based on Numbers

A convergent city school of 600 secondary school students has some 20 teachers supervising 20 homerooms of 30 students each. Of the 600 students, approximately 300 are males. Any youths from outside the school can be recognized as such, and any youth from within the school who commits a crime can be recognized by name or at least described to other teachers to find out his or her name. The 1% of students who are most difficult to control number only 6 and are not numerous enough to take over the school.

A divergent metropolitan school of 3,000 students has some 100 teachers supervising 100 homerooms of 30 students each. The number of males is 1,500. In a school of this size, it becomes very difficult for the teachers to recognize who does and does not belong. Thus youths from outside the school are difficult to recognize as such, while those from within the school who commit a crime may be difficult to identify. The 1% who are most difficult to control numbers 30 students, a sufficient and critical number needed to form a gang or otherwise interfere with education and security. The consequence is loss of control in the large school of the divergent metropolis when compared with its small counterpart of the past.

Activity Participation

Important research on school size was carried out by Roger Barker and Page V. Gump and published in *Big School, Small School* (1964). These researchers found an interesting paradox: Even though large schools offer many more extracurricular activity choices than do small schools, small schools obtain significantly higher levels of student participation.

Barker explains this result in terms of "undermanning." A small school's few activities are short of members and actively recruit more. For example, a school of 500 students has to involve 5% of them in order to fill a football roster of 25. This means that one does not have to be a talented athlete to participate.

A school of 3,000 needs to involve less than 1% of its students to fill that same football roster. This is why the small school, with fewer choices, absorbs a higher proportion of its students into the system of informal development and control. If the goal is to involve young people (not to win a championship), the small school wins out. From a control theory viewpoint, small schools are far superior in tying young people into society by including them in conventional activities.

Barker and Gump do not deny that large schools have the advantage of offering a greater variety of activities. This is consistent with their advantage in offering a greater curricular variety because there are enough students to fill different types of classes and hence to offer more of them.

Control Factors
Based on Buildings and Grounds

The small school of the convergent city is compact enough to provide significant control. The relatively few halls and stairwells are easy to watch. The principal's office could be located strategically on the first floor to check those who enter; the three- or four-story design ensures that an office by the ground floor entry could prevent illegal intrusions. The lack of landscaping affords no place to hide illegal behavior. The compact grounds are easy to supervise and serve to increase the number of teachers per acre, which in turn enhances security.[3]

In contrast, the large school of the divergent metropolis is more spread out and thus not amenable to easy control at entry points. With many more hallways, nooks, and crannies, knowing who belongs there is a tougher problem. Extra landscaping helps to hide illegal behavior. With spacious school grounds, a small number of teachers per acre reduces control.

Evidence That Large Schools
Bring More Crime

The link between school size and crime is clear. Larger schools have higher crime rates (correcting for the effects of size alone). Thus a school five times as large might have 10 times as much crime. The significance of school size for crime in the United States is found in the Safe School Study (U.S. Department of Education, 1978; see also Gottfredson & Gottfredson, 1985); similar research for Britain is found in Hope (1982). That research also verified that more landscaping and more acreage contribute to more crime.

We should not treat school crime as a trivial matter. In the 1989 National Crime Survey, 2% of students reported violent victimizations at school, and 7% reported property victimizations. These are very high victimization rates when compared to national levels. Moreover, assaults on teachers were significant in some schools examined in the Safe School Study. In addition, Dennis Roncek's research found higher crime rates on those residential blocks where public high schools are located. This means that schools produce crime not only on their own sites, but also in nearby areas.[4] In addition, school crime impinges on other community problems, such as achieving racial integration, which is more than an arithmetic trick.

Large Schools and Racial Integration

The large urban school impairs meaningful racial integration, although such schools make it easy for a school board to achieve apparent integration. It is relatively easy to bus 1,000 children of one race to a school with 2,000 students of another race, thus meeting legal requirements, and declare that school to be integrated. Integration is formally defined by courts on a whole-school basis, not a social interaction basis. However, massive schools tend to impair meaningful informal contacts across racial boundaries. Within such schools, one quickly observes strong racial segregation among students when they sit down in the lunchroom, when they socialize before and after school, and when they enroll for specific classes or curricula. Thus racial segregation continues under the guise of integration. We may refer to this as *pseudointegration*, because it satisfies formal criteria of integration while maintaining racial segregation in practice.

Having 3,000 adolescents of any color under the same roof defies common sense; trying to obtain meaningful interracial contact in such a setting is even more difficult. Enlarging schools may achieve pseudo-integration by meeting a formal goal, but it misses the point of breaking down social barriers.

Worse yet, the large school puts the most aggressive and hostile members of each race in a position to dominate the situation simply because their sheer numbers reach a critical minimum (a point made earlier). Their ability to dominate the situation can show up either in racial conflict or cooperative interracial delinquency. In either case, the large school is no friend of meaningful interracial education. All the large school does is produce pseudointegration while making "officially integrated" school boundaries easier to draw.

Summary

This chapter compares the small school that is typical of the convergent city with the large school common in the divergent metropolis. In comparing numbers of students as well as the size and characteristics of buildings and grounds, we have argued that the large schools of the divergent metropolis undermine control. This reasoning is consistent with empirical evidence that large schools bring greater risk of crime than the small schools of the convergent city. Indeed, the large school makes it possible for youths to escape adult control and to develop settings dominated by adolescents. The following chapter discusses how the divergent metropolis in general makes possible this same loss of control on an even larger scale.

Questions for Writing, Reflection, and Debate

---

1. Suppose that you are principal of a large school. Can you think of any ways to increase informal control given the school with which you must work?

2. From a crime prevention standpoint, what is the optimal size for elementary school? For secondary school?

3.   Which of the points in this chapter also apply to the size of a college or university?

Sources for Ideas

Many of my ideas are derived from Barker and Gump (1964), who detail the daily activity patterns of students. They show that small schools absorb students more effectively into activities than do large schools. Barker has a unique empirical tool: the behavior setting. He divides a town into many behavior settings and monitors human activities in terms of time spent in these settings.

I was also intrigued by Gottfredson and Gottfredson (1985). This well-written volume contains a wealth of detail on school disruption and control by making use of the Safe School Study. The authors confirm the disruptive effects of large schools. They offer a variety of other administrative advice for improving school security, along with the educational environment in general. Their main recommendation is to hire better principals. I prefer a structural change, taking school organizations as given and attempting to set up schools whose size brings out the best abilities of all participants from students to principals.

The British study by Hope (1982) confirms my argument that schools with the most trees, facilities, and space, however pleasing to parents, tend to produce more crime. This paper is available through Butterworths, the publisher, and is found in various U.S. libraries. It is consistent with the U.S. Department of Education's *Safe School Study* (1978) but adds more.

Endnotes

1.   For statistics on school size, see the 1989 *Statistical Abstract of the United States*, Table 219. For urban and rural school statistics over time, see annual editions of the *Digest of Education Statistics* and *Statistics of Public Elementary and Secondary School Systems* (both from the U.S. Department of Education). School size also is discussed at great length in Barker and Gump (1964).

2.   That social control in schools is influenced by size is a point made in Gottfredson and Gottfredson (1985) and in U.S. Department of Education (1978). Also see McPartland and McDill (1976, 1977); a strong argument along similar lines is presented in Garbarino (1978).

3. School design and crime is taken up in Hope (1982). See also Crowe (1990) and Crowe (1991), especially pages 162-170. A review of the more general topic of schools and crime is found in Toby (1983).

4. High school effects on crime in the vicinity is explored in Roncek and Lobosco (1983). A more personalized approach to the role of schools in fostering or preventing crime is that of Olweus (1978).

7

Filling Time, Avoiding Crime

Observe any meetings of people,
and you will always find their eagerness and
impetuosity rise or fall in proportion to their numbers.

—*Lord Chesterfield (Letters to His Son, September 13, 1748)*

The quality of a life is determined by its activities.

—*Aristotle (Nicomachaean Ethics 1.0, trans. by J. A. K. Thomson)*

This chapter examines changes in the recreation between the convergent city and today's divergent metropolis. We describe (a) a shift of recreation away from household and family settings and (b) an impoverishment of outdoor urban recreation as pedestrian street life declines in the divergent metropolis. We begin by examining youth activities near parental settings.

Changing Activity Patterns for Youths

In 1979, the Illinois Reminiscence Survey gathered some interesting indicators of a dramatic change in adolescent activity patterns over several generations. Telephone interviewers contacted a sample of the Illinois population aged 18 and older, asking respondents to think back to age 17 and describe their routine activities in some detail. This interview was quite popular with interviewers and respondents alike and quickly was nicknamed "The Summer of '42" survey after an old movie.[1]

Responses indicated dramatic changes in activity patterns over the generations, with much more parental control over the older generations of teenagers, especially females. To begin, bedtimes of 11 p.m. or later were reported among only 17% of males and 9% of females who had turned 18 in 1940 or before. In comparison, for those who turned 18 in the 1971 to 1979 period, approximately half of both sexes reported going to bed routinely at 11 p.m. or later. However, later bedtimes cannot alone establish declines in parental controls. We asked much more direct questions about activities of youths occur and their locations compared to adults:

> When you were 17, was a parent or another adult relative with
> you on Saturdays always, most of the time, some of the time, or never?
> By what time were you usually required to be back home on
> Friday nights?

If the response was "No definite hours," our interviewers then asked:

> By what time were you usually expected to be back home on
> Friday nights?

The same questions were asked for Saturday nights. We call the responses the "bewitching hour" (see Table 7.1).[2]

Respondents who were 17 years old at some point in the 1971 to 1979 period were more than twice as likely to be away from parents on Saturdays as those who were 17 in 1940 or before. We also observed an increase in the bewitching hour from a median of 11:36 p.m. for males in the oldest group to 1 a.m. for males in the newest group. For females, the corresponding change was from 10:44 p.m. to 12:24 a.m. In another question (not shown) respondents indicated that they went out more nights, both during the week and on weekends.

We also estimated the proportion of 17-year-olds who were away from home at each hour for the average Friday and Saturday night, based on respondent reports of how often they were out as well as how late they returned. For both sexes there are major changes, but female changes are especially noteworthy. In the oldest group, only 13% of females would be out past 11 p.m. on the average Friday or Saturday night. For the newest group, this increases to 83%, more than five times what it had been. Significant portions of the female population aged 17 are also out past midnight.

When we asked whether an adult was present when the respondent was out with friends after dark, one fourth of the oldest group of males said yes; this figure declined to only 8% in the most recent group. For females, the corresponding change was from one in three to one in four.

Several other interesting questions were asked:

> When you were 17, on weekdays did you have any regular
> household chores or duties to perform in the afternoon?

Table 7.1 Weekend Activities Remembered at Age 17 (Four Groups)

Year Turned 18	Not With Parents on Saturday (%)	Saturday Bewitching Hour	Estimated % Out Friday, Saturday Night Past	
			11 p.m.	Midnight
Males				
1940 (and before)	26	11:36 p.m.	30	7
1941-1960	42	12:35	52	15
1961-1970	45	12:42	68	29
1971-1979	59	1:00 a.m.	73	43
Females				
1940 (and before)	16	10:44 p.m.	13	2
1941-1960	18	12:11	40	10
1961-1970	33	12:14	42	12
1971-1979	42	12:24	83	13

Base *N* ranges from 31 to 94

Source: Felson and Gottfredson (1984)

Between 3 and 6 p.m. on weekdays were you at home always, most of the time, some of the time, or never? (If "never," skip next question).

When you were at home between 3 p.m. and 6 p.m. on weekdays, was an adult there with you?

Did all of the members of your household usually eat the evening meal together on weekdays?

For both males and females, approximately half of the more recent respondents had no afternoon chores, a major increase in "freedom" over the older group (see Table 7.2). There were also increases in the numbers away in the afternoon; when young people are home in the afternoon, adults are increasingly absent.

Perhaps the most interesting finding is that the family dinner together, nearly universal in the older group, declined noticeably for the younger group. I have asked this question of my students in several classes in recent

*Table 7.2 Daily Routines (in Percentages) of Young People at Age 17
Near Their Parents*

	Males		Females	
Year Turned 18	1940, before	1971-1979	1940, before	1971-1979
No afternoon chores	31	51	28	48
Seldom home*	43	66	22	50
Adults not present*	15	40	5	30
Evening meals together	94	63	97	75

*Never or sometimes
Base *N* ranges from 27 to 93

years and find an even more extreme change, with very few reporting family meals together as usual weekday events.

In sum, both weekdays and weekends saw increasing independence of teenagers from parental settings. This conclusion is underscored by several questions about driving. We first inquired whether the respondent had a driver's license at age 17. In the oldest group, 57% of males said yes; this response increased to 79% in the most recent group. For females, the same question found changes from 20% to 65%. We view this as a dramatic turnaround in control of teenagers. Major changes were also reported in driving often after dark and riding with other teenagers after dark. Again the greatest changes were for females.

Perhaps the most eye-opening calculations stem from the following thought experiment. Suppose that two boys wish to get together and smoke marijuana. To do so they have to have the right circumstances, away from parental control. Ideally, neither will have chores to do in the afternoon, neither will have to be back home for family dinner, or to be back with parents on Saturday. Both should be able to ride around after dark and stay out late.

Now if we pick two boys at random, what is the probability that neither will have to be home for afterschool chores? Noting that 31% in the oldest group have no afternoon chores, we can multiply .31 × .31 to find that there is only a .09 probability that neither boy will have an afternoon chore. Because 51% in the more recent group have no afternoon chore, we can multiply .51 × .51 to learn that there is now a .25 probability that both boys will be free. We can see clearly that freedom from parents increases.

We have shown evidence of a shift in adolescent activities in one state. These findings are quite consistent with the overall national pattern of increased teenage driving and empty households. The next section links the observed patterns to the development of the divergent metropolis.

The Divergent Metropolis and Adolescent Activities

As stated in Chapter 4, the divergent metropolis disperses people over more households, housing over more space, travelers over more vehicles, and activities away from family and household. These features contribute to less control of adolescents.

Supervising the Home Itself

In describing the change between the convergent city and divergent metropolis, three elements are especially important for the control of adolescents: (a) mothers outside the labor force,[3] (b) mothers without automobiles, and (c) diverse relatives sharing the same household.

When mothers were out of the labor force, they were home more and better able to watch the household and what went on there. Having no automobile meant staying closer to home. With additional relatives such as grandparents sharing the household, that space was even more likely to be supervised both day and night. In the divergent metropolis, these control factors are largely absent. With increasing numbers of households unsupervised in the daytime, teenagers have many more opportunities to escape parental controls, both when using home for their own purposes and when going elsewhere.

Youths per Acre

Because the divergent metropolis has fewer children per household and fewer households per acre, the net effect is very few children per acre.[4] To find enough others one's own age to set up a basketball or football game becomes difficult. It would be good if the older children graciously invited the younger children to join their games and if the boys would invite the girls to join as well; but more likely they will separate into smaller groups.

The lack of robust recreation activity perpetuates the crime problem by providing fewer guardians in parks and on the streets. Youths are diverted into legal activities for too few hours per week, leaving too much time on their hands in settings in which adults are nowhere to be found.

After-School Activities

With school over at 3 p.m. and working parents returning at approximately 6 p.m., an afternoon vacuum of at least three hours must be filled. Even if school activities keep a young person occupied for an extra hour, two thirds of the afternoon vacuum remains unfilled. Parents who lack the money to pay for extra activities will not find it easy to fill this vacuum. With nobody home to cook dinner, a family meal together is impractical. Modern appliances serve to reduce chores at home (see Chapter 5), and it becomes less necessary to assign lengthy chores to teenagers and to insist that they stay home to do them.

The Role of Automobiles

Automobiles intrinsically provide greater autonomy to their drivers. This point applies especially to adolescents, who gain from automobiles a great opportunity to get together away from family and household activities.[5]

The dramatic spread of drivers' licenses for youths make such convergences easier. But a more important factor is the increasing number of families with several cars. In the 1940s most families had no car at all. In the 1950s families typically owned a single car, which the father used to go to work and parents diverted to family uses and their own social purposes on weekends. Teenagers were low on the pecking order when it came to car use, needing to find evenings when parents were not using the car. Teenage siblings had to compete for use of a single car.

Perhaps most important, a single car gave a family a greater chance to go out together. Even teenagers, faced with the choice of staying at home with nothing to do or going out with parents, might choose the latter. Moreover, a single car produced family planning of activities. For example, parents might drop a son off at a friend's house, a daughter off somewhere else, go to a party, and then pick up the two children on the way back. Trips such as these provided mild parental supervision of the timing and location of the childrens' activities.

Compared to the one-car family, the two-car family more than doubled adolescent access. If parents were going out together in the evening in one car, that still left the other car for one of the teenage children. A three-car family would have an extra car for two teenage children, even if one car was reserved for parents in the evening.

As the number of family cars increases, family activities together tend to decline, while careful family timing of automobile use falls by the wayside. Each family member of driving age could now select a personal itinerary, making it more difficult for parents to verify where their children are going to or coming from. The automobile puts parents in a bad position: The very structure of society makes it difficult to deny automobiles to their children, and yet providing their children cars to drive increases their risks of getting into trouble as offenders or as victims of crime, not to speak of traffic accident risks. Moreover, increased adolescent mobility makes neighborhoods more difficult to watch. One's own children not only are farther from home, but also one can less readily tell which youths or adults live here or there, which are just visiting, or which have illegal intentions.

In the divergent metropolis, bus service gets weaker, especially on evenings and weekends when social life most needs transportation. Declining densities make distances greater and walking less efficient. Heavy and fast automotive traffic is no friend to pedestrians or bicycles. As cars become virtually the only option for getting anywhere, youths too young to drive are increasingly dependent on parental chauffeuring.

Parental Efforts to Arrange Activities for the Young

Given the structure of the divergent metropolis, parental efforts to organize activities for their children become difficult and expensive.

The Swedish Comparison

In Sweden, the government assumes that all mothers work and so provides a program to help mothers with their children.[6] In each neighborhood, *Fritid* is the free afternoon activity provided for children after school. Its purpose is to keep children occupied from the time school is out to the time parents arrive home. The program, designed for preteen-agers, is paid for by Sweden's high taxes. At the age when one is old enough to participate in delinquency, the program is not applicable. For teenagers, Sweden has roughly the same problem we do, except that its teenagers lack automobiles and must rely on public transportation. Be-cause Swedes live in housing clusters at higher density than most Ameri-cans and have much better public transportation, youths can get around in the afternoon and evening. This makes it easier for them to participate in legitimate activities and to socialize, but it also helps some of them to find opportunities for delinquency.

How Youth Programs Can Backfire

Americans have a long history of organizing recreation for young people, often with the idea of preventing delinquency. However, such recreation programs for youth have a spotty history in preventing crime. An example is Malcolm Klein's (1971) report of a program organized by adults for delinquent gangs.[7] Klein's research on gangs has found that most of them are loose, disorganized, and intermittent. He found that the program kept gangs going longer than those in a control group who had no such program. Far from weaning young people away from gangs, the adult program provided a focus for gang activities, giving the gangs extra cohesion and longer life.

Recreation programs can backfire by assembling likely offenders who might not have gotten together otherwise. Recall the vacuum period between the time school lets out and the time parents arrive home. Recreation programs should be careful not to assemble young people and then dump them out in small groups into the community after the adults go home. On the way home, youths may engage in vandalism, shoplifting, or other illegal activities or provide personal or property targets for other youths. Covering only part of the afternoon vacuum leaves the rest of it available for delinquency. Moreover, youths who are not expected to be home at any particular time can easily get involved in crime when the program is over, even if the program lasts a few hours. The simple fact that adults organize recreation does not guarantee crime prevention.

Parentally Organized Youth Sports Leagues

Every Saturday in Autumn, approximately 100 nine-year-old boys on teams of 25 each play two peewee football games in a park in Champaign, Illinois. Some 100 cars fill the parking lots. These games are part of an elaborate league that is organized by adults just to provide one practice and one game per week for their children. During the rest of the week, the same park is largely empty.

Several points are illustrated by this example:

◆ This recreation depends on parental chauffeuring. Indeed, a million dollars worth of automobiles are needed to produce two peewee football games.[8]

◆ Considering all the effort that goes into this, very little time is actually spent playing football, which makes it hardly adequate for meeting recreational needs or for making very good football players.

◆ Judging from the empty park, young people in this area do not seem to be able to arrange and play football without parents helping.

Episodic Recreation
in the Divergent Metropolis

Culture and night life have found adaptations to the divergent metropolis.[9] The first adaptation is to concentrate all activity on weekends. Advertising is generally needed to contrive a crowd at a specific location. Large crowds and high prices are generally necessary to pay for advertising and for locations that are highly active for a few hours but inactive for the rest of the week. Such entertainment depends on large parking lots and produces small and sporadic streams of pedestrians. The parking lots are suitable for theft of or from automobiles. Those stragglers who leave the place of entertainment too late may find themselves walking where there is no ongoing flow of pedestrians to serve as guardians against a personal attack.

Summary Thus Far

So far in this chapter, we have presented survey evidence of the changing activity patterns at age 17, and we have reviewed many of the recreation

patterns of the divergent metropolis. These patterns provide many opportunities for those with money to spend but very few recreational options
at little or no cost. Episodic events can be organized and crowds contrived.
Youth programs can be planned and sometimes succeed. However, streets
and youths are not naturally occupied.

We finish this chapter by recalling again the convergent city and reveal-
ing more of its recreation patterns. The comparisons underscore why the
divergent metropolis continues to lack something important.

A Comparison:
Recreation in the Convergent City

To understand better the limitations of the recreation programs just mentioned, we need to remind ourselves of the more natural recreation
patterns of the convergent city. Several features of the convergent city
produced high densities of informal recreation and street activity.

High Population Density

The convergent city's high population density filled streets and parks with
pedestrians. This crowding provided its own recreation: Because people
like to look at each other, just walking around or sitting and watching the
street could be entertaining. The large number of youths per acre helped
to produce activity.

In addition, most people lived in crowded apartments or tiny row
houses, with little recreation space. People depended on streets and city
parks to get away from home. Because the pedestrian density consisted
largely of local people, individuals would likely be recognized and thus
discouraged from criminal behavior.

Pedestrian traffic and localism combined to produce many chance
encounters of old friends, plus the opportunity to meet new people
through them. This added to the incentive to stay on the street while it
increased the risk for someone acting against the law to be recognized by
someone else. Thus the convergent city provided "natural" social life
along with "natural" surveillance.

City parks were generally small and crowded. Street corners were
crowded with people "hanging out," and people congregated in other
public places such as pool halls and bars. Thus sidewalks and parks in the

convergent city were crowded with pedestrians of various ages, leaving adolescents subject to mild and informal scrutiny by adults.

Outside of work and school hours, games of basketball, football, stickball, or softball grew spontaneously, drawing from the high density and young age structure. Such games continued for hours on end, changing participants in the process. Younger or weaker players commonly waited on the sidelines to substitute for preferred players as they left the game to go home or to late-shift jobs. A passing pedestrian might join in. Children gravitated there on their own on a daily basis and did not require parents to deliver them.

Heavy pedestrian flows could also be found in central entertainment districts of convergent cities. People would walk or take public transit to the entertainment district in the evening. The streams of people would provide customers for vaudeville and other live theater, movie theaters, restaurants, and the like. It was common to go to movies several times a week, and Hollywood produced cheap films by the thousands in response. Entertainment was an ongoing activity, pedestrians an ongoing flow. The crowd and entertainment fed one another.

The heyday of New York City's Broadway was in the era of the convergent city. Thousands of people walked along 42nd Street and in Times Square, going to the theater or just looking at one another. This activity made possible the era of musical comedy, the great compositions of Lerner and Loewe, the Gershwins, Rodgers and Hart, Rodgers and Hammerstein, Jerome Kern, and others. The pedestrian flows and bar hopping also made possible a great era of jazz improvisation, with music going every night of the week. This is an interesting example of how the ordinary begets the extraordinary. Ordinary settings favorable to artistic exploration in time produce creativity and brilliance. This is far better for creativity than occasional special concerts.

Armies of pedestrians in the convergent city provided customers for street vendors, just as street vendors provided an extra reason to be a pedestrian. Fruit, vegetables, clothes, newspapers—all were available from street vendors. Many shops set up tables just outside their doors. Activity was oriented to the street. A newspaper vendor could survive in that era selling his sole product for a few cents each to thousands of pedestrians. This was the lifeblood of big city newspapers. It also encouraged people to read newspapers in parks and in front of buildings. The street vendors, newspaper boys, newspaper readers, and pedestrians together provided ample guardians for the streets and parks of the convergent city. Whatever the convergent city's problems with pickpockets and grab-and-run attacks on merchants' wares, the more terrifying forms of street crime were difficult to carry out among so many guardians. Even when business trailed off there would usually be enough people on the street to prevent overt criminal attacks.

Filling Time and Timing Crime

This chapter has demonstrated how the divergent metropolis has altered the patterns of filling time in comparison to the convergent city. This alteration applies to both youths and adults. The divergent metropolis reduces the age-sex diversity of daily interaction and often assembles male youths free from any adult supervision. Activities move away from home to settings with sparse and sporadic pedestrian activity. The result is a lack of ongoing recreation with natural guardianship against crime. To compensate, people contrive settings to meet their recreational needs. These contrivances restore the lost recreation only in part and add more crime in the process.

Questions for Writing, Reflection, and Debate

---

1. You are a parent trying to arrange to keep your teenage children out of trouble. What is your plan? What are the pitfalls to be avoided?

2. Administer the Illinois Reminiscence Survey to some young people today and compare the results to Tables 7.1 and 7.2.

3. What are the relative advantages of a convergent city or divergent metropolis at ages 5, 15, 22, 45, and 65?

4. As youths gain freedom from parental controls, do parents also gain freedom? Do parents then begin to behave less responsibly?

Sources for Ideas

Many ideas about a convergent city's outdoor life are found in Whyte (1988). This is an interesting collection of observations about people in Manhattan, including how people walk, how design of outdoor spaces impels or impairs social life, and how dense cities bring something out in people that we do not find in suburbs.[10] For an account of micro-environmental differences in everyday life, see Michelson (1976). With many photographs and sketches, the author shows how different micro-environments affect everyday behavior in cities.[11] Differences between multifamily and single-family dwellings are taken seriously.

For a better understanding of how situational features enter our daily lives, see Bandura (1985). Although he does not provide the ecological engine to explain how "chance encounters" are organized, his thinking is solid and applies to many topics including crime.

An interesting book on adult recreation in cities is Ostransky (1978). This volume describes jazz in New Orleans, Chicago, Kansas City, and New York City. Despite the author's clear love for jazz, he makes no effort to hide the symbiotic relationship between the jazz scene and the gangster scene. This book clearly links the music to specific quarters in the city.

Endnotes

1. To request a copy of the questionnaire for the Illinois Reminiscence Survey, please write the author:
   Marcus Felson
   Social Science Research Institute
   University of Southern California
   Los Angeles, CA 90089-1111

2. The issue of memory and earlier ages is taken up in sources cited in Felson and Gottfredson (1984). For more on adolescent activity patterns, see Greenberger and Steinberg (1986) and Bahr (1980). The general thesis of the dispersion of activities away from family and household is found in the work of William F. Ogburn, most easily accessible in *On Culture and Social Change: Selected Papers* (1964). See also Ogburn and Nimkoff (1955).

3. For more information on married female labor-force participation trends, see the household change section of Chapter 1 and its citations. For evidence of empty daytime households during the same period of change (e.g., the 1960s), see U.S. Bureau of the Census (1973).

4. Youths per acre can be calculated from age data and land area for metropolitan areas in 1950, 1960, 1970, and 1980; the figures can be estimated for 1986 and 1987. See U.S. Bureau of the Census (1950, 1960, 1970, 1980a, 1980b) and the 1989 *Statistical Abstract of the United States*, Table 32.

5. For a general source on the transformations resulting from the automobile, see Gilmore (1953).

6. The Swedish information was gathered by the author during his sabbatical there.

7. For more on the uncertainty of recreation and crime prevention, see Hirschi (1969), pages 187, 189-190.

8. The peewee football example should be compared with statistical work on joint time spent by parents and children; see Medrich, Roizen, Rubin, and Buckley (1982).

9. The episodic recreation of the divergent metropolis is best seen by comparing what we see today to New Orleans in the past; see Ostransky (1978).

10. Suburbanization is taken up in Jackson (1985) and Fishman (1987).

11. Background on the daily activity and recreation patterns of the convergent city can be gathered from Deutsch (1951), Milgram (1970), Whyte (1988), Booth (1902), and Salisbury (1984). On pedestrian life and the social life of the street, see Barker (1963), Goffman (1963), Lofland (1973), and Sommer (1969). On street corners, see W. F. Whyte (1961). Also see W. H. Whyte (1988) for numerous passages about topics such as parks, streets, play areas, retailing at street level, selling entrances, and the like.

8

Natural Crime Prevention

Who will not judge him worthy to be robbed
That sets his doors wide open to a thief,
And shows the felon where his treasure lies?

—*Ben Jonson (Every Man in His Humour, 1598, 3.3)*

To keep oneself safe does not mean to bury oneself.

—*Seneca ("On Peace of Mind," Moral Essays, trans. by Aubrey Stewart)*

In 1961, Jane Jacobs' classic book *Death and Life of Great American Cities* documented the tragedy of urban renewal before anyone else realized what was happening. She explained why old urban neighborhoods, even if low in income, provided places for pedestrians, had vibrant lives, maintained local control of space, and protected people against crime. These neighborhoods were bulldozed to erect unnatural high-rise public housing complexes that became sterile environments and which had crime problems built into their design. Jane Jacobs remains a hero to students of crime prevention because she showed us how designing more crime is as easy as designing less. Her concept went beyond buildings themselves, including the entire urban environment and taking into consideration people using that environment. Her spark of creativity and freshness of thought might have enlightened U.S. crime policy for decades to come.

However, that was not what happened. Leadership fell into the hands of naive ideologies, first liberal and then conservative. The first proposed to reduce crime by assuming that if government is good to people, then they will be good in return. The second proposed to reduce crime by assuming that if government is bad to people, then they will be good in return. Had either or both camps listened to Jane Jacobs, they would have realized that the issue is not how good or bad the government is to people but whether public places are designed and organized to allow people to control their own environments informally.

Around 1970, two other opportunities arose for crime policy to incorporate common sense. C. Ray Jeffery invented "Crime Prevention through Environmental Design" (CPTED; pronounced "sehp-tehd"), to which we devote a large part of this chapter (Jeffery, 1971). And Oscar Newman (1972, 1980) contributed landmark books about crime prevention, using such terms as *defensible space, natural surveillance*, and *community of interest*. Newman explained how crime could be prevented by creating buildings, environments, and communities that provided for interaction with and influence against crime.

Unfortunately, in the United States most public agencies have had little knowledge about or interest in designing out crime, preferring instead to wait until crime happens and then punishing the few people that can be apprehended. Nor is the academic world a center of interest in practical prevention. U.S. business has a much more enlightened attitude than government or universities, putting a good deal of effort into preventing crime by keeping offenders away from targets or otherwise reducing crime opportunities (see the section below on retail prevention). Among researchers, the most creative bundle of prevention projects began within the British government's civil service system.[1]

Situational Prevention: Experiments and Innovations

Great Britain's Home Office is roughly equivalent to the U.S. Department of Justice. Within this agency was the small Research and Planning Unit, located during the 1970s at Romney House on Marsham Street, a five-minute walk from Scotland Yard. There in 1973, Senior Research Officer Ronald V. Clarke had just completed a study of why youths abscond from borstals (American translation: why juvenile delinquents run away from reform school). In this study, the usual social science variables did not successfully explain the phenomenon. However, when Clarke took a look at the day of the week on which these events occurred, he found that most boys ran away on weekends when staffing and supervision were light. Because these were not prisons and staff members were not guards, their influence was more informal. Merely by being present, adults could prevent a certain amount of trouble, including absconding.

With these results, Clarke began to think of crime in general as the result of human situations and opportunities. In 1976, with Pat Mayhew, A. Sturman, and J. M. Hough, Clarke published *Crime as Opportunity*, and Clarke later became the unit's head. Under his leadership, several British researchers inside and outside the government created or discovered real-life crime prevention experiments. They adopted the following policy.

- Do not worry about academic theories. Just go out and gather facts about crime from nature herself (that is, by observing, interviewing offenders, etc.).

- Focus on very specific slices of crime, such as vandalism against telephones or soccer violence.

- Try to block crime in a practical, natural, and simple way.

They called their efforts *situational prevention*. From the 1970s to the present, many remarkable situational prevention studies have been carried out. A crime prevention unit was also established, and the two units contribute much of the systematic crime prevention work now available. We will now look at how the simple approach of situational prevention has been put into successful practice.

Trouble on Double-Deck Buses

We begin our illustration of situational prevention with the problem of vandalism against Britain's traditional red double-deck buses. The Home Office researchers (Clarke, 1978) learned that most of the vandalism was on the upper deck, usually in the back row, where supervision was least likely to occur. They also learned that the traditional British bus conductor had a major role in preventing vandalism. A bus conductor would ascend the stairs to the upper deck to collect fares and thus serve as a guardian against the crime of vandalism. One experiment put conductors back on buses that no longer had them. The experiment succeeded in reducing vandalism but had an unexpected result: Conductors were assaulted more often. This is an example of how crime prevention can sometimes backfire, solving one crime but leading to another. This also establishes that situational crime prevention is far from obvious, sometimes producing unexpected results.

Car Theft Prevention

Another interesting example of how crime prevention policy may not work quite right is seen in Great Britain's efforts to thwart car theft.

A Home Office study by Pat Mayhew, Ronald Clarke, and Mike Hough (1992) examined the impact of steering wheel locks on car theft. This study compared British experience with that of the former Federal Republic of Germany. Whereas the British enacted a law that only required steering wheel locks on new cars, the West Germans required that *all* cars—even old cars—have such locks installed by a certain date. In the British case, car thieves diverted their attention away from new cars and stole older models that lacked steering wheel locks. Thus the overall car theft rate did not decline. In West Germany, the more comprehensive law produced a dramatic reduction in car theft across the board. This lower risk held for subsequent years.

This study indicates first that crime prevention can be accomplished without significant displacement to other crimes or other victims. Second, it teaches us that avoiding such displacement requires making some crime prevention efforts universal rather than piecemeal.

Motorcycle Theft Prevention

If the West German success in the case of car theft resulted from careful thinking, the same nation was successful with another crime prevention measure entirely by accident.

The West German government enacted a law that required motorcyclists to wear helmets to prevent serious injuries from accidents. After police began to enforce the law, the thefts of motorcycles declined precipitously. Many motorcycle thefts are for joyriding and occur on the spur of the moment. A youth who saw a shiny motorcycle and was suddenly tempted to steal it would usually not happen to have a motorcycle helmet and would decide not to commit the theft.[2]

Several lessons can be learned from this example. First, we see that significant crime prevention can occur completely without planning. Second, the example demonstrates that fairly simple changes in rules or laws can have major significance for crime prevention. Third, we see that highly visible behavior (in this case, wearing a helmet while riding a motorcycle) can help produce controls. Fourth, this example found no evidence of displacement of prevented motorcycle crime to other vehicle thefts.

The two German vehicle theft examples achieved crime prevention by means of across-the-board laws enacted centrally. However, some crime prevention requires more "personal service," as the next example suggests.

Burglary Prevention

When Ken Pease (1992) studied burglary in British public housing, he noticed that some units were burglarized repeatedly. So when someone's home was burglarized for a first time, a prevention team focused its efforts on that particular unit to prevent a repetition. The team enlisted the residents of the five or six homes nearest the burglarized unit to keep an eye on it. The result was a lower burglary rate. The unit's success was far greater than the usual generally unfocused and ineffective Neighborhood Watch in the United States.

So far we have offered only British examples of situational prevention. Similar well-focused crime prevention is found in the following U.S. example.

Subway Graffiti in New York City

For many years, the subway trains of New York City were covered inside and out with ugly graffiti, surely among the ugliest anywhere.[3] Moreover, the transit system was in chaos, ridership was dropping, and employee morale was low. Many efforts and policies had failed to correct the problems.

Then David Gunn became president of the New York City Transit Authority and announced the Clean Car Program. The aim of the program was to clean off graffiti immediately. This is important because it gave the graffiti painters no satisfaction in seeing their work travel around New York City. This removed the incentive and gave them no more reason to paint graffiti on subway cars. Compared to its previous experience, New York City's subway cars became largely free from major graffiti problems as a result of this program. One lesson of the program: Find out exactly what the offenders want and why they commit a particular crime. This information will guide the design of countermeasures.

Another subway system far distant from New York City prevented graffiti in fixed locations using a very different plan.

Graffiti in Swedish

The Swedish government publishes a pamphlet for tourists, "The World's Longest Art Gallery—The Stockholm Metro."[4] More than half of Stockholm's 99 metro stations have artwork, and more than 70 artists have contributed underground caves, mosaics, paintings, engravings, and wall reliefs.

Do not expect this subway art to win prizes for art. However, if there were a Nobel Prize in graffiti prevention, the Stockholm Metro should win it. Resistance to graffiti was achieved with five techniques:

1. The use of multicolored art means that a graffiti painter would need many different cans of paint to cover the art.
2. Highly polished surfaces are difficult to paint on.
3. Very rough surfaces are hard to paint on and make it hard to read what has been painted.
4. Sharply uneven walls (such as those in a cave) are not suitable for painting a readable message.
5. Metal grills block walls and offer too little surface for a painted message to show.

The examples so far have demonstrated prevention of property crimes. However, it is also possible to prevent violent crime.

Preventing Football Violence

British football (soccer) has an unfortunate pattern of serious and sometimes fatal violence.[5] Many fans arrive hours before a game, get drunk, and then commit acts of violence, many against fans of the visiting team. Because most of those involved in violence own no cars and take buses to the games, the government arranged for these buses to arrive later than in the past, allowing only a few minutes to buy a ticket and no time to get drunk. The effect was a reduction in football violence.

Sweden also has a problem containing violence, at least on one day each year.

Channeling Revelry

Midsummer's Day (usually June 21) is the longest day of the year. In much of Sweden, this day has 24 hours of light. It is the most important holiday of the year. Swedes are usually reserved people, but they make an exception on Midsummer's Eve. A common behavior pattern is to get drunk and run wild. People also burn bonfires, which sometimes get out of hand and burn more than intended. Moreover, many assaults occur on Midsummer's Day.

The crowds are far larger and wilder than anything police can handle, so deterrence loses its credibility. A more sensible policy was planned by Swedish authorities: They provided bonfires in designated and advertised locations and sought to channel the holiday spirit into these settings. Their efforts paid off by reducing assaults and other illegal behavior (see Bjor, Knutsson, & Kuhlhorn, 1992).

The next example deals with channeling crowd behavior of a different type.

Cruising Cooper Street in Arlington, Texas

In many European and Hispanic nations, young people walk around the center of town on weekend evenings. The U.S. version of this activity is cruising in cars. But cruising creates traffic jams and interferes with business. The automobile spreads adolescent activity over more space and makes it harder to prevent trouble; thus vandalism and assaults become more serious. Many U.S. cities have enacted special cruising ordinances or enforce traffic and parking ordinances more heavily in trying to control cruising.

As explained by authors John Bell and Barbara Burke (1992), the city of Arlington, Texas, found that cruising by more than 1,000 cars was creating a major traffic jam on its main street for hours at a time. Ambulances could not get to hospitals and little else in the way of normal city business could happen. Conventional traffic control methods were doing little good.

City Councilman Ken Groves learned that teenagers wanted two things: (a) an unstructured and unsupervised environment in which to mingle and (b) rest rooms. He speculated that if these were provided, most teenagers would act reasonably. A "cruising committee" was formed to link local agencies, business, the University of Texas at Arlington, and teenage representatives.

The committee devised a plan for the city to lease a large parking lot from the university and open it to cruisers on weekend nights while providing unobtrusive police protection, portable rest rooms, and cleanup the next morning. Within two weekends, the new cruising area was in use by 1,000 parked or circling cars. The program channeled cruising into a smaller and safer area and pleased both teenagers and adults, while providing the gentle controls of a few police officers on the side. The lesson of the program is that a crime problem may be related to another problem; solve the other problem and the crime problem takes care of itself. In this case, the problem was to provide youths with a social need in the context of the local situation. This was done and the related crime problems dissipated. (We will discuss problem-oriented policing later in this chapter.)

The Displacement Issue

Displacement occurs when the crime prevented in one setting shifts to another setting (see Barr & Pease, 1990). The goal of prevention is to reduce overall crime, not merely for one area to dump its crime problem onto another. In the steering wheel lock research, the motorcycle study, and other studies not presented here, Clarke and his associates have been able to demonstrate little or no displacement to other crimes or other settings when situational prevention is carefully conceived and executed.

We have offered several examples from different nations to demonstrate the utility of situational prevention not only in helping us think about crime prevention but also in finding real solutions to specific crime problems. We now turn to a more strategic and comprehensive approach to crime prevention: designing better environments.

Crime Prevention
Through Environmental Design

A husband-and-wife team at Simon Fraser University, Pat and Paul Brantingham, began an important crime prevention effort in Vancouver, in the western Canadian province of British Columbia. This is an area with roughly the same climate and "feel" of Seattle, Washington.

Here the Brantinghams developed and applied CPTED (invented by C. Ray Jeffery). Forging relationships with local architects, planning boards, and police, they helped apply CPTED in many settings. One of the most interesting developments in British Columbia is that the Royal Canadian Mounted Police began to train its officers in CPTED. For example, these "Mounties" are trained to read blueprints; they routinely sit on planning boards, examining detailed plans for new construction and making suggestions to help reduce the risk of crime. As a result, many new housing complexes, businesses, and schools in British Columbia apply principles of CPTED from the outset.

The following are examples of the sort of useful advice that these British Columbians can offer about crime prevention:

- Keep schools well away from shopping malls, so youths do not flock to the malls after school or at lunch time and become involved in theft, vandalism, and drug use.

- Make sure that school lunches are provided either at school or in local institutions with adults near, so youths do not go "out on the town."

- Plan carefully the routes that teenagers walk from housing developments to local high schools and back. Make sure these routes do not cross parking lots and thus invite vandalism against cars.

- When constructing public housing, make sure it is low-rise; avoid vast unassigned public space; avoid walls or solid fences that give burglars something to hide behind.

- Design housing for the elderly as a high-rise building with a glass-walled recreation room on the first floor. Thus the residents can keep watch on the doors.[6]

Although this British Columbian approach does not conflict with the spirit of the British approach, there are some differences in emphasis. As Table 8.1 indicates, situational prevention focuses on a specific slice of a crime problem, plans in a more targeted fashion, acts more directly, involves business more than public agencies or police, reflects a psychological origin, and is linked to a "rational choice" theory of crime. This theory is summed up in the title of one of its books, *The Reasoning Criminal*, which examines how the offender thinks about a crime situation. By

Table 8.1 Situational Crime Prevention Versus CPTED

	Approach	
	British Situational Prevention	**British Columbian CPTED**
Focus	specific crime problem	local environment
Planning concept	targeted	comprehensive
Action concept	act directly	act more indirectly
Police involvement	minimal	substantial
Work more with	business	public agencies
Origins	psychology	urban planning
Theoretical basis	rational choice	environmental criminology

learning more details about the offender's thought processes, we might be able to figure out how to thwart illegal action before it even starts.

The British Columbian approach uses CPTED, acts more indirectly, pays attention to comprehensive planning of local environments, and substantially involves public agencies and police. This reflects its origin in urban planning and is manifested in its theoretical term: *environmental criminology*. This theory has contributed the "geometry of crime" (described in Chapter 2), which traces an offender's normal route from work to school to home to entertainment. By planning locations of homes, schools, and recreation areas before a community is actually constructed, environmental criminologists can help to reduce crime levels in the community.

Although CPTED principles should be applied well before an environment is constructed, it is very often too late: The building already stands and a serious crime problem needs to be corrected. Sometimes changes can still be made to improve the situation. Here is a good example from across the Atlantic.

A Shopping Mall and Drug Market

The Netherlands combines the quaintness of dikes and windmills with some of Europe's highest population densities and crime rates. The Dutch Ministry of Justice has established local crime prevention offices and encouraged them to develop their own crime prevention projects. An interesting case in point is the effort to reduce a major crime problem in Utrecht's central-city shopping mall. There young drug addicts were hanging out, buying and selling drugs, using drugs on the premises, and committing predatory crimes in the vicinity. The authorities redesigned the mall to remove dead space and hidden corners, and they blocked private parts of the mall (such as service areas and offices) from public access.[7] The effect of these efforts was neither to "wipe out crime" nor to displace crime to other locations. However, it did put a lid on the crime problem and helped reduce its worst manifestations.[8]

Several examples so far have considered planning fairly large parts of a community. The following example demonstrates that it is possible to plan several components of quite a very limited environment: a small store.

Reducing Convenience Store and Small Grocery Robberies

Small stores with late hours are very vulnerable to robbery, especially when located near freeways. In some cases employees or customers have been injured or murdered in the process. One large convenience-store chain, 7-Eleven, suffered staggering increases in the numbers of robberies during the 1970s. The chain's owner, the Southland Corporation, hired several convicted robbers, including Ray Johnson, and the Western Behavioral Sciences Institute to help redesign the corporation's retail stores with the intention of reducing the number of holdups. Sixty stores initiated the team's recommendations, and a control group of the same size did not. The control group experienced no change in robbery risk, while the experimental group had a 30% decline in the number of robberies. These stores also reported major declines in nearby crime and in people loitering and harassing customers. The following are the stores' main innovations.

1. Display advertising that once covered all windows was removed so that would-be robbers would feel that they were more easily noticed from the street and thus subject to guardianship.

2. Cash registers were moved to the front of the store, making them visible from the street.

3. Both registers and clerks were placed on a raised platform. This took the cash drawer out of the offender's line of vision and reduced temptation.

4. Special timed-access safes were placed beneath each register. These safes take in cash, especially large bills, but can release no more than $10 change every two minutes. This removed the target of the crime by making most of the money inaccessible.

5. Store properties were redesigned to eliminate all alley exits and to channel traffic to and from the streets out front. This helped customers better serve as guardians for one another.

6. Taxi drivers were encouraged to use the premises as a nighttime station at no cost and with free coffee and rest room privileges. This provided mild surveillance of the area at little cost.

7. Employees were trained to make eye contact with each customer on entry. This provided a more informal social influence against crime.

These 7-Eleven crime prevention policies have had the net effect of making stores more comfortable and safe for employees, customers, and neighbors, while avoiding the use of armed guards.[9]

With the urging of Professor C. Ray Jeffery, the city of Gainesville, Florida, placed similar stipulations into a city ordinance and also required the presence of at least two clerks on duty late at night. The result was a decline in convenience-store robberies.

In most of our examples, crime prevention was the main motivating factor for the planning effort. Yet Tim Crowe of the National Crime Prevention Institute argues, "Good planning is good prevention and good prevention is good planning."[10] His point is that a well-designed environment accomplishes its basic goals and simultaneously serves to prevent crime. Applying this principle to a small grocery or convenience store, a good design will not only reduce crime but also produce a better store in which customers enjoy shopping. No better illustration of this principle can be found than in the next example.

Disney World Is No Fantasyland

Clifford Shearing and Phillip Stenning (1992) have reported how Disney World organizes your visit in great detail. From parking lot to train to Monorail to park and back, activities are planned to minimize risk of accident or crime. Disney World follows this rule: Embed control in other structures so that it is barely noticed. For example, there is only one way to get into many exhibits: within a vehicle controlled by Disney personnel. Even when people are waiting in line, their wait is structured by railings that wrap each line of people back and forth. This encourages informal conversations and proximity of people in different age groups, thus reducing impatience and discouraging rowdiness by youths.

The most important lesson of Disney planning is that almost all visitors to Disney World are quite contented with the way their visit is managed and voluntarily comply. (Of course, people are not spending the rest of their lives in Disney World.) The lessons of this example are that crime prevention can be most effective when it is incidental, and that a well-planned and well-managed environment serves many human purposes along with security.

Preventing Retail Crime

Along the same lines, George Luciano, an expert in retail crime prevention, argues that good management and crime prevention go hand-in-hand within retail stores.[11] A well-managed and well-organized retail store has many good features, including more sales and fewer losses to shoplifting or employee theft.

Retail stores use many prevention methods. More frequent inventories and audits help to discourage employee thefts. Requiring that all merchandise be bagged and stapled makes it harder for a customer to slip something unpaid for into his or her bag. Tags that beep when not deactivated discourage shoplifters. Designing exit routes carefully encourages people to pay for their merchandise as they walk out. Electronic systems for detecting merchandise are increasingly available at low price, paying for themselves in loss reduction within a year or two.

Retail stores can easily lose thousands of dollars worth of clothing in a few seconds to two or three people who grab stacks of expensive garments and run to a waiting car. Stores also can easily lose tens of thousands out the back door. The well-managed store combines comprehensive planning with situational prevention to prevent such losses. An example of comprehensive planning is the careful scheduling of deliveries so that the back door is under supervision. An interesting example of situational prevention is to put the hangers for expensive garments on the rack in alternating directions. Thus when a grab-and-run thief tries to pull them off, they lock in place. This small but ingenious idea is clearly superior to letting people steal and then waiting for the criminal justice system to find and punish them.[12]

From Many Specific Examples, a Few General Principles

We have seen contributions to crime prevention from Great Britain, Canada, the Netherlands, Sweden, the former West Germany, and the United States. Some of these efforts focus on specific crime problems (situational prevention), and other efforts focus on settings (CPTED). With either philosophy and in many different contexts, we repeatedly return to a simple but powerful idea: Crime can most often be prevented by following nature as closely as possible. This means avoiding so far as one can the use of the criminal justice system, armed guards, violence, and threats. Instead, we prefer to set up situations and environments in which acting legally feels like the normal and comfortable thing to do.

We call this *natural crime prevention*. It avoids a walled-off society and seeks more sophisticated means for avoiding crime. Those who construct walls around their backyards may not realize that this method has a tendency to backfire. Once an intruder has entered, the solid wall provides him with a screen for committing crime freely. Natural crime prevention suggests much less forbidding fences, affording significant visibility and thus reducing the temptation to intrude in the first place. For similar reasons, natural prevention recommends trimming hedges and the lower branches of trees so that offenders cannot readily conceal themselves.[13]

Nor are guards with uniforms and guns necessary in most applications. It usually makes more sense for unarmed people to inquire politely, "May I help you?" when they notice someone wandering around with no legitimate purpose or for a receptionist or doorkeeper to offer assistance and thus provide a kinder, gentler, and subtler form of security.[14]

Natural crime prevention includes (a) unplanned and informal crime prevention as it occurs naturally in everyday life and (b) planned crime prevention that imitates the former by skillfully designing human settings or activities so that crime opportunities are unobtrusively and nonviolently reduced.

One central theme of crime prevention in this chapter and throughout this book is that crime prevention works more naturally when human activities are divided into smaller and more manageable chunks. These chunks can help provide social control and thus crime control. For example, cars and motorcycles can be made more conspicuous when stolen so that local people can notice what has happened and do something about it. Responsibility to stop burglary can be linked to those in the immediate area. A school can be situated for more local visibility, and public housing can be designed or sized for better control. High-rise buildings can be arranged so that elderly people can protect their piece of the world. A shopping area, too, can be localized for more control. Even wild holiday activities can be localized for greater security of those involved.

Just as activity can be chunked, so can it be channeled. Teenagers can be channeled away from places where they will get into trouble and over routes where mild supervision can be provided. Disney World channels its thousands of visitors per hour to minimize conflict. Cruising on weekend nights can be channeled to minimize crime while improving the social nature of the activity. Retail stores can channel customer and employee activity to discourage theft.

These examples lead us to an *informal* description of our approach to prevention:

> Natural crime prevention may be described as the chunking and channeling of human activities, in imitation of nature, to reduce crime temptations and increase controls.

We have offered examples of such prevention from various settings in several nations. These examples and those from previous chapters provide some ideas for new crime prevention efforts.

Agenda for the Future

Many institutions in society can do much to reduce crime.

Improving Youth Programs

To begin, government and school programs for youths need to think more clearly about supervision aspects. We began Chapter 7 by discussing an adult-sponsored program for gang members that actually created more crime, and we ended Chapter 5 by discussing the failure of jobs for youths to reduce crime. In light of these disappointments, we need to consider how youth programs could be designed more effectively for crime prevention. We suggest that youth programs can improve their chances for success by shifting to a tangible, situational definition of what is needed. A government jobs program for youths should be structured more carefully, locating jobs in mixed-age and mixed-sex settings, away from opportunities to commit employee theft, and with arrangements to go home after work. Afterschool activities for youths should seek to follow these same rules as well as fill most of the afternoon vacuum (see Chapter 7).[15]

What Schools Can Do to Reduce Crime

Another area of policy disappointment is the limited success schools have in keeping youths out of trouble (see Chapter 6). Again we need to think more carefully about school activities as they are located in time and space. For example:

- start and end school later each day so that it more closely corresponds to parental work schedules,
- include more of the summer period within the school year,
- avoid excessive parks and landscaping right next to schools,
- keep smaller schools alive, and
- discourage "open campuses" where secondary school students can enter and leave at any time.

These suggestions are all designed to help restore natural and informal social control to schools and nearby settings, both during school hours and afterward.

What Colleges and Universities Can Do to Reduce Crime

Even though a campus is already built, it can make relatively small changes with surprisingly large consequences for security. A campus can:

- trim hedges and lower branches of trees,
- design out blind corners and block off less used parts of parking structures when there is no special need for them,
- put movement-sensitive lights in remaining blind spots,

- improve sign-in procedures for visitors to student housing,
- locate receptionists in places where they can better see who enters,
- assign security responsibility to someone in each building or section of a building,
- install new locks or key mechanisms on doors used more often and limit key distribution,
- provide bicycle racks and get people to use them properly,
- organize bicycle-check areas and provide attendants, and
- improve window protection to prevent illegal entry.

Gather the facts on a specific security problem before acting. For example, exactly *why* are graduate students or employees blocking the security doors open? Find out and then solve the problem rather than simply posting a sign demanding that they cease blocking the doors. In short, find the facts, use common sense, and do not be too conventional. Students who follow these rules can probably produce a better plan than anybody else for reducing crime on campus.

What Industry Can Do to Reduce Crime

Important contributions to natural crime prevention can be made by industrialists in the future.[16] Even before products arrive at the store, they can be designed and manufactured in ways that reduce crime.

Clarke and Harris (1992) list numerous technical changes that the auto industry can contribute to help reduce auto theft:

- mark various valuable parts around the car with serial numbers;
- install high-security locks for steering column, doors, and hood;
- use flush-sill buttons that are difficult to pull up with a clothes hanger;
- strengthen window glass so that it is harder to break;
- protect the internal door-latching components;
- install hood-release catches; and
- program an audible reminder to remove keys from the ignition.

More expensive cars can also offer central locking and, when a break-in occurs, immobilize the engine through its electronic-management system.

The story of the Chevrolet Corvette provides a most interesting example of what the industrialist can do for crime prevention. Once the most stolen car in the United States, it now offers a small resistor embedded in the ignition key. When the key's resistance does not match the car's decoder, it cuts off the fuel injectors and the starter. This disables the car for awhile. Only an electronics-sophisticated thief can defeat the system, which even then requires 15 minutes.

British Rover eliminates external door locks entirely, using an infrared transmitter to open the door instead. If windows are broken, this immobilizes the ignition system. The car's entertainment system is security coded; if removed, it can only be activated by a personal identification number.

Going beyond the automobile industry, inexpensive technology already exists to put a personal identification number into every new and valuable electronic item, such as a television set or videocassette recorder. The product will not work outside your home unless this number is entered. An item thus will be of no value to the thief. Industry can make a major contribution to society by designing and selling products that "go kaput" when stolen (see Felson, 1987b).

What Police Can Do to Reduce Crime

Herman Goldstein (1990) has coined the term "problem-oriented policing." Arguing that the goal of policing should be to reduce crime, not simply to arrest people, he has suggested first figuring out specific problems that need to be attacked and then targeting police action toward those problems. For example, if a drug house is generating most of the crime in an area, then it should be the target of action. The first step would be to find out who owns the property and make that person aware of what is going on there. Sometimes the landlord is willing to put an end to the problem by not renewing a lease.

In some cases, a drug dealer does business next to a pay phone, taking orders on the phone and handing drugs to customers as they drive by to pick up their orders. The police and the neighborhood can get the phone company to change the phone so that it will only call out and not receive calls, thus driving this specific illegal market out of business.

Many other examples and a good deal of experience is accruing in police departments and among other public agencies working with them. U.S. police are beginning to follow the example of the Mounties in seeking innovative opportunities to reduce crime. However, they are having some difficulty getting their minds off of arresting people. Will problem-oriented policing end up meaning nothing more than "targeting arrests"? Or will police begin to include in their repertoire a vast array of ideas for natural crime prevention? We hope that in another few years our critique of police effectiveness in Chapter 1 will be obsolete.[17]

Summary

We have seen that crime prevention can be introduced incrementally into many parts of our society. The basic strategy is to imitate activity patterns of everyday life as already observed in nature. Included are chunking and channeling human activity to reduce temptations and increase informal control. Such efforts can reduce crime, up to a point, given the context of our current society. The next chapter considers how new technology could provide a much more significant reduction in crime by changing the structure of our society more fundamentally.

Questions for Writing, Reflection, and Debate

---

1. Describe the college campus with which you are most familiar in terms of its spatial flows of students, staff members, and outsiders. Where are students and staff members most likely to be at risk of having their property stolen?

2. Discuss Ronald V. Clarke's argument that many examples of situational prevention lead to no displacement. What are the implications of this assertion for the nature of crime and criminals? Accepting the implied nature of crime and criminals, when should we expect displacement and when not?

3. What are the relative advantages and disadvantages of preventing crime through comprehensive planning of a whole area (advocated by the Brantinghams) versus situational prevention (advocated by Clarke)?

Sources for Ideas

Many of this chapter's ideas have been drawn from Ronald V. Clarke, *Situational Crime Prevention: Successful Case Studies* (1992). This volume includes 22 case studies of successful crime prevention projects in Britain and other countries, including the United States. It offers the easiest way for the student to get hold of many of the world's best studies, along with the best list of references and best index for crime prevention projects. Many of these studies cast doubt on the argument that preventing crime here will merely displace it there. See also Clarke (1983).

Those who are interested in cars and car theft should see Clarke and Harris (1992). This paper is the penultimate review—everything you ever wanted to know about auto theft and how to stop it. It is more than a review, for its concepts help us to think clearly and carefully about the many events that contribute to car crime and the many approaches to prevention.

A leading source in the crime prevention field is Barry Poyner. His *Design Against Crime: Beyond Defensible Space* (1983) is an outstanding collection of examples and advice for specific designs to prevent crime. Two of Poyner's prevention projects are also included in Clarke's case studies (above).

I have also been influenced by Paul and Patricia Brantingham's edited volume, *Environmental Criminology* (1990). See Chapter 1, "Notes on the Geometry of Crime," by the editors themselves. They show how the movements of offenders and victims in space bring them together. Beginning with the simplest case, they develop increasingly sophisticated understanding of these movement patterns. Although their consideration of work trips is external to the factory or office, the same principles can be easily applied to movements within the workplace, bringing offenders into contact with personal or property targets.

Endnotes

1. See Mayhew, Clarke, Sturman, and Hough (1976). For reviews of the British efforts, see the bibliography in Clarke (1992), Clarke's (1983) review article, and Poyner (forthcoming). The theoretical basis for the British work is found in Cornish and Clarke (1986).

2. On motorcycles, see Mayhew, Clarke, and Eliot (1989).

3. On subway graffiti in New York City, see Sloan-Howitt and Kelling (1992).

4. Storstockholms Lokaltrafic (Greater Stockholm Metro) (no date).

5. On football violence, see Clarke (1983).

6. For an excellent summary of the Brantingham and British Columbia crime prevention in action, see Brantingham (1989). The theoretical basis for this work is found in Brantingham and Brantingham (1991).

7. In addition, the Utrecht Police Department created a special police task force for the shopping center. Their duty was to get to know every youth by name and make sure they knew the officers by name. They made it clear to the youths what lines they could not cross (such as using drugs on the premises) and that they had to keep moving. When officers enter the mall, they say hello to each "client" (which is how they refer to an addict) and introduce themselves to any new ones. Social services are provided through a social worker hired by the police department.

8. The Netherlands example was gathered from a mall tour given me by the Utrecht Police Department. A review of Dutch crime prevention efforts is found in Van Dijk and Junger-Tas (1988).

9. The convenience store robbery reduction example is reported by Duffala (1972); see also Hunter and Jeffery (1992).

10. The quote is from personal communication, but see Crowe (1991).

11. George Luciano's comments were from a personal interview.

12. On preventing retail crime, see the bibliography and review in Geason and Wilson (1992), as well as Hayes (1992). U.S. business is much better at preventing crime than writing about it. For this reason, the Social Science Research Institute at the University of Southern California has been funded by the National Institute of Justice to gather crime prevention information from people in many walks of life (the Crime-Free Environments Project, grant 91-IJ-CX-KO21.) The results will be the topic of another book.

13. Natural crime prevention wishes to avoid a walled off society; note how burglars operate in Bennett and Wright (1984). On closing streets, see "Judge Disallows Gates" (*Los Angeles Times*, 1993). The ease of discouraging most criminals is illustrated in Cromwell et al. (1991); the burglary informants were reluctant to target a home when a few children were around.

14. Contributions of the doorman and concierge to crime prevention fit the argument that armed guards are generally not necessary.

15. The agenda for youth programs should be examined in light of Greenberger and Steinberg (1986).

16. The agenda for industrialists to prevent crime by design is drawn from Clarke and Harris (1992) as well as from Southall and Ekblom (1985) and Geason and Wilson (1990).

17. On police change, see Goldstein (1990). See also Toch and Grant (1991), Moore (1992), and Eck and Spelman (1987).

9

Into the Future:
Community and Safety Regained?

Astronomers work always with the past;
because light takes time to move
from one place to another,
they see things as they were,
not as they are.

—*Neale E. Howard*
(The Telescope Handbook and Star Atlas, 1967, p. 3)

A rock pile ceases to be a rock pile
the moment a single man contemplates it,
bearing within him the image of a cathedral.

—*Antoine de Saint-Exupery*
(Flight to Arras, 1942, p. 22, trans. by Lewis Galantiere)

The roots of the future are in the present. Although we cannot be sure of the future, we can at least take a look at these current roots and how they are growing, hoping to draw some inferences about what is to come. These inferences may help us to anticipate crime in the future.

To help us along in this task, we draw from two visions of the future that were offered two and three decades ago and which remain interesting.

A Tale of Two Visions

In 1973, E.F. Schumacher contributed the best-selling book *Small Is Beautiful: Economics As If People Mattered*. In it he chronicles many problems produced by large organizations and advanced technologies. He argues forcefully for smaller organizations and simpler technologies. A basic assumption of his book is that smallness and technological simplicity go together.

Another influential book appeared in 1962, Marshal McLuhan's *The Gutenberg Galaxy: The Making of Typographic Man*. According to McLuhan, "The new electronic interdependence recreates the world in the image of a global village" (p. 31).

Mass communications play a central role in this interdependence. As computers and telecommunications have developed to even higher levels of complexity since McLuhan wrote three decades ago, "global village" has become the watch phrase of many technology writers.

McLuhan recognized that human beings have community needs, which he expressed as "tribal." Accordingly, he noted, "the sealing of the entire human family into a single global tribe" (p. 8); "our new electric culture provides our lives again with a tribal base" (p. 32).

The visions of McLuhan and Schumacher surely contrast greatly. The first vision offers a simple and localized world with minimalist technology, while the second sees a global world based on advanced communications. Yet both authors have a common notion that human beings need communal bonds to one another.

Three decades have passed since McLuhan's book and two decades since Schumacher's. Enough change in North American society has occurred to allow a comparison of their visions with what actually happened.

What the Data Show

Both technological sophistication and size of work organizations are indeed changing in the United States. Let us first examine recent trends in sales of advanced electronic equipment in the United States as an indicator of technological sophistication.[1] As Table 9.1 indicates, such sales have increased more than fivefold in a dozen years to more than $73 billion. These sales data clearly indicate, consistent with McLuhan, a more technologically sophisticated world. Other data show a proliferation of international telephone calls, supporting McLuhan's and Schumacher's forecast of increased global communications.

Next we consider smallness in the workplace. We examine the distribution of the U.S. labor force by the size of the establishments at which people work, such as the number of people working in a given office or factory.

There were about 60 million jobs in 1975 and 83 million in 1986. As Table 9.2 shows, the percentage distribution of these jobs shifted toward smaller

Table 9.1 U.S. Sales of Computers, Peripheral Computer Equipment, and Industrial Electronic Equipment, 1975 to 1987

Year	Sales ($ billion)
1975	13.5
1978	26.0
1979	32.8
1980	39.5
1981	47.8
1982	54.9
1983	58.1
1984	69.6
1985	70.1
1986	68.4
1987	73.3

Source: *Statistical Abstract of the United States* (1989), Table 1312

establishments. Those with 20 to 99 employees showed the greatest gain. Meanwhile, establishments with more than 500 employees declined in size, and those with more than 1,000 declined the most in their share of the total jobs. In only 11 years, the larger establishments lost a noticeable share of the labor force, falling 23.4% to 19.8%. Establishment size is a basic structural feature of U.S. society, which usually does not change that much that quickly. Thus a fascinating combination of social change is occurring in the United States: more complex technology with smaller workplaces.[2]

Interpretation

We find that our visionaries were each half-right and half-wrong in stating what would or could happen. Schumacher correctly foresaw a growth in small organizations but was quite off the mark if he expected less sophistication in technology.[3] On the other hand, McLuhan was quite accurate in expecting enhancement in technology and communications linkages, but the declining size of work establishments was not part of his thinking.

These results lead us to reject Schumacher's linkage between technology and smallness. It appears that smallness can grow despite high

Table 9.2 Changes in Labor Force Distribution, 1975 to 1986

Total Number of Employees per Establishment	Percentage of Total Businesses		Percentage Change
	1975	1986	
Fewer than 20	27.1	26.7	−0.4
20-99	26.9	29.2	+2.3
100-499	22.6	24.3	+1.7
500-999	8.0	6.9	−1.1
1,000+	15.4	12.9	−2.5
Totals	100.0	100.0	
Base jobs	60,519,000	83,380,000	

Source: *Statistical Abstract of the United States* (1990), Table 860

technology. A case can be made for an even more interesting interpretation: High technology makes smallness more possible than ever before! Desktop computers, business software, beepers, cellular phones, fax machines, laser printers, voice mail, overnight delivery across the nation—all make it easier for small businesses to operate in our society. Modern machine tools that can be reprogrammed quickly make it easier for a small factory to operate and compete. Lightweight plastic and aluminum parts and products assist the spread of light manufacturing to smaller sites. Given our shift to a service economy, the spread of computers and networks among computers makes it easier to provide services from a small- or medium-sized office.

What we see in Tables 9.1 and 9.2 is *sophisticated smallness*. Small organizations offer and use sophisticated services; they purchase high-technology computer equipment and software and plug into advanced information systems.

Smallness and Localism

Smallness implies localism; localism implies control. As opposed to a few large workplaces, many small work establishments can be located (a) in more places and (b) near residential areas. With workplaces closer to home, even though most people will still have to get up and go to work,[4] they will have a shorter commute and be able to get home sooner after work.

Many commuters will be able to leave work early, pick up their children at school, spend time with them, and then work on the home computer.[5] We can see that activities moving closer to home can help to enrich community life. As more people travel within their local area, they are more likely to recognize one another. This increases informal social control and reduces the crime problem. In short, if sophisticated smallness indeed characterizes our society in the future, we can expect a basis for lower crime rates. Smaller schools could also contribute to localism.

Education in Smaller Packages

Many of the same technological developments that facilitate small business and small factories can help U.S. society rediscover small schools. The next section takes one innovation as a case in point.

Telecourses

Two problems sometimes find a marriage that produces a solution for each. Here is an example.

Problem 1. Two high schools each have 15 students who want to take a course in criminology. One has located a local criminologist to teach the class, but the school actually needs 30 students for the class to be viable.

Problem 2. Telephone capacity is increasing vastly because of fiber optics, which carry messages at the speed of light. To use this excess capacity, telephone companies have developed a clear television screen that covers an entire wall and methods to send a picture for this screen by fiber optics. Their problem is that they need customers for this developing service.

Solution. Telephone companies are beginning to develop this market by adapting this technology for telecourses. A teacher teaches one half of a class live at Location A, while a televised wall behind these students displays the other half of the class from Location B. The students there see a wall in front of them with the backs of the heads of the students at Location A, plus the teacher facing students at both locations. If the students at Location A turn around, they see their fellow classmates at Location B. Thus all students at both locations feel like they and their teacher are in the same classroom, while the teacher has the sensation of teaching a single class. The fiber optics transmit questions, answers, and discussion instantaneously.[6]

Telecourses can breathe extra life into small schools. They can also enable community colleges and local extensions of large universities to offer specialized courses. College students whose jobs, families, or residences prohibit travel to a distant campus can attend nearby telecourses. A single telecenter can draw on professors from many colleges and universities, or a business can set up its own telecenter to help its employees supplement their training. The new technology is far superior to today's teleconferences.

The important point is that this new technology meets real human needs. It helps people simplify their lives, reduce their expenses, avoid unwanted trips, and gain learning and sophistication within smaller organizations, in a classroom setting, while staying close to home.

Technology does not change our lives simply by being remarkable. It must help us do something that is important. The prototype for telecourses has already been demonstrated in Illinois. As organizations work out the practical details, this innovation can begin to serve educational needs closer to home.

Warming Up Computers

Working alone on the computer is not always self-motivating. However, recent developments are beginning to warm this technology to meet human needs. Multimedia systems combine videotapes, music tapes, games, and computer interaction. All they need to do is add taste, touch, and smell to meet all five human senses. Far from a means for isolating human beings from one another, the computer can become a means for linking them together in the learning process.[7]

Our general point is that machinery begins to change society the most after it is perfected and dominated by people and forged to meet their specific human needs. That is why we should not evaluate the social importance of technology until people have seized it for human purposes. In 1915 those who watched a driver crank up an automobile by hand might never have guessed that this machine could radically change society. In 1950, those who used an early computer that filled a whole room might not have expected much of the cybernetic age. We have to use our imagination to project from today's incipient technology what changes are in store for society.

Even today, using computers requires much more expertise and training than we can expect in 10 years. To force computers into a human mold, scientists are developing ways to communicate with them more simply. Special screens already allow students to answer a question or make a request simply by touching the computer screen itself. Other computers respond to voice commands, and scientists are working on ways to make computers recognize speech commands with fewer errors. Computer recognition of handwriting is also under development. As it becomes easier to tell a computer what to do, the machines can do more to educate people to work for them without experts needing to be nearby.

We are making future projections based on technology as it is now developing. Ours is a five-step argument:

1. Computers and new communications media increasingly do what nonexperts want them to do without experts nearby and with fewer breakdowns and quicker service. They fit human ways of thinking and acting more closely, while helping people to interact. In short, computers and communications are getting "warmer."

2. These new technologies are available to organizations of every size as well as to individuals.

3. Thus a large school loses its advantage over a small school in the variety of learning it can offer.

4. Yet a large school continues to have greater problems of social control.

5. Hence the large school loses its edge.

Why go to a large school with extra crime problems if the large school no longer offers a practical curricular advantage over the small school? Indeed, if schools get smaller, they will also tend to get closer to home. With smaller, localized schools and businesses, we can expect community life to grow stronger.

Closer to Home

American society is slowly resolving the problems it created. At the outset for experts, computers became incrementally easier to use. Lightweight electronic goods fed a crime wave, but these items can now be programmed to disable themselves when stolen. Educational television was cold and lackluster, but new technology humanizes it. Armies of bureaucrats marched daily toward their central files; today's small and scattered offices draw instantly from even more immense computer files.

If the automotive age gravely weakened the local community, the newest technologies now make it possible to live, work, shop, and matriculate within a narrower span of territory on a daily basis. With shorter daily commutes, families can spend a little more time together. As organizations get smaller, natural crime prevention at the workplace becomes more practical. As daily activities are focused into less space, local people will more often recognize one another and thus contribute informal social control. With activities closer to home, Americans will at last have a chance to combine the ingredients to produce what so many of them want: prosperous, sophisticated, livable, and safe metropolitan environments.[8]

Questions for Writing, Reflection, and Debate

1. What impediments remain for the small office and small school, even given new information technologies?

2. What developments in computer software could help schools to get smaller?

3. For the moment, take the author's thesis as correct. In what order do you think that various organizations will get smaller?

Sources for Ideas

For an easy-to-read book that tells us why technology often upsets people and what can be done to design things that are usable and likable, see Donald A. Norman, *The Psychology of Everyday Things* (1988). The author helps us to think about everyday things (and he really means "things") from a designer's viewpoint, but he also helps a designer think about things from a user's viewpoint. This author is not fooled by new technology for its own sake; an innovation should not be fancy and it should help the user in his or her everyday life.

The most important sources for technology information from a practical viewpoint are in the technology sections of newspapers and business publications or technology news in the business sections of newspapers. Such sources are much more practical and less technical than scientific or industry sources. Examples are *Business Week*, *The Economist*, the *Los Angeles Times*, the *New York Times*, and the *Wall Street Journal*. See also *Computerworld*, *Electronic Media*, *Technology Review*, *Telecommunications Update*, and *Satellite Week*.

Endnotes

1. In addition to Tables 9.1 and 9.2, see U.S. Bureau of the Census (1974, 1986), Table 1b; citations are based on Table 1c.

2. Examples of technology combined with smallness is found in Flanigan (1993, p. 1). To quote: "[Y]ou can see the effect of buzzwords like technology and infrastructure in Gray and Boones Creek, Tenn., small towns in the Great Smoky Mountains, where computer record-keeping for Sears Roebuck's credit operations provides new jobs thanks to the spread of advanced telecommunications lines and equipment."

3. In drawing this simple comparison between Schumacher and McLuhan, we should note that each is more interesting and sophisticated than this simple characterization. For example, Schumacher does not dogmatically call for small organizations. At some points in his book (e.g., pages 65 and 242) he takes a much more flexible approach, which I shall paraphrase in the next few sentences. He states that human activities simultaneously require freedom and order: the freedom of a multitude of small, autonomous units and the order of large-scale coordination. Action requires small units because it is difficult to be in touch with many people at once. Indeed, Schumacher surprises us (p. 64) by praising General Motors President Sloan for arranging a gigantic firm as a federation of smaller ones. The appropriate size of an organization depends on your purpose. For some purposes small units are needed, and for other purposes large units are appropriate: "For every activity there is a certain appropriate scale, and the more active and intimate the activity, the smaller the number of people that can take part" (p. 66). He further explains: "The fundamental task is to achieve smallness within large organizations" (p. 242). Despite these interesting remarks, Schumacher makes clear that his preference is for smallness and that the burden of proof is always on those who prefer large organizations. He appreciates the fact that human organization can be large-scale in one respect and small-scale in another respect. This possibility has a chance to develop to a far greater extent with new information technologies developing as they are. Small-scale units can be plugged into large-scale networks of communication and cooperation or command. The local units may still complain about the boss or the central headquarters. However, from a crime prevention viewpoint, small local units permit activities to be closer to home and to be monitored more naturally

within the work setting itself. Thus outsiders can less readily intrude into offices to steal wallets or computers. Insiders can less easily wander to different departments to act illegally against fellow employees, clients, or employers. Parents can get home more quickly and interact more with their children, meanwhile paying closer attention to the neighborhood turf.

4. Note that I have rejected the home office as the dominant form of activity in the future. I think smaller, more local offices are the likely form of work organization because people are too tempted and distracted at home to work effectively there and need to share the interactions and contacts of the office setting.

5. It makes sense even today to begin a task at the office, consulting with people face-to-face, and then to finish that task at home. This permits some blending of face-to-face consultation for work purposes with face-to-face requirements of family life.

6. My source for the telecourse information is an engineer involved in the project. For other essays on communications technology and social change, see Kochen (1989).

7. On warming up computers, the technology is changing so fast that it is almost pointless to give citations that would be obsolete within a month. See "Sources for Ideas" at the end of Chapter 9 for periodical sources.

8. On continuing changes in the metropolis, see Barnett (1989). Also note U.S. Department of Transportation (1992) and Downs (1989).

References

Akers, R. L. (1984). Delinquent behavior, drugs and alcohol: What is the relationship? *Today's Delinquent, 3*, 19-47.

Akerstrom, M. (1993). *Crooks and squares: Lifestyles of thieves and addicts in comparison to conventional people.* New Brunswick, NJ: Transaction Books.

Ambrose, S. E. (1984). *Eisenhower: Soldier, general of the army, president-elect, 1890-1952.* New York: Simon & Schuster.

Argyle, M., Furnham, A., & Graham, J. A. (1981). *Social situations.* Cambridge, UK: Cambridge University Press.

Assembly of Behavioral and Social Sciences. (1978). *Deterrence and incapacitation: Estimating the effects of criminal sanctions on crime rates.* Washington, DC: National Academy of Sciences.

Bahr, H. M. (1980, Spring). Changes in family life in Middletown, 1924-1977. *Public Opinion Quarterly, 44*, 35-52.

Bandura, A. (1985). The psychology of chance encounters and life patterns. *American Psychologist, 37*, 747-755.

Barker, R. (1963). *The stream of behavior.* New York: Appleton-Century-Crofts.

Barker, R. G., & Gump, P. V. (Eds.). (1964). *Big school, small school.* Stanford, CA: Stanford University Press.

Barlow, H. (1990). *Introduction to criminology* (5th ed.). New York: Harper-Collins.

Barnett, J. (1989, Spring). Redesigning the metropolis: The case for a new approach. *American Planning Association Journal*, pp. 131-135.

Barr, R., & Pease, K. (1990). Crime placement, displacement and deflection. In M. Tonry & N. Morris (Eds.), *Crime and justice: A review of research* (Vol. 12, pp. 277-318). Chicago: University of Chicago Press.

Beavon, D. J. (1984). *Crime and the environmental opportunity structure: The influence of street networks on the patterning of property offences.* Unpublished master's thesis, Simon Fraser University, British Columbia, Canada.

Bell, J., & Burke, B. (1992). Cruising Cooper Street. Chapter 7 in R. V. Clarke (Ed.), *Situational crime prevention: Successful case studies.* New York: Harrow & Heston.

Bellot, S. (1983). *Portrait du voleur à main armée occasionel* [A portrait of the casual armed robber]. (Technical Report No. 7). Montreal: International Center of Comparative Criminology, University of Montreal.

Bennett, T., & Wright, R. (1984). *Burglars on burglary: Prevention and the offender.* London: Gower.

Bentham, J. (1948). *The principles of morals and legislation.* New York: Hofner.

Berry, B. J. L., Cutler, I., Draine, E. H., Kiang, Y., Tocalis, T. R., & de Vise, P. (1976). *Chicago: Transformations of an urban system.* Cambridge, MA: Ballinger.

Beunen, G., & Malina, R. M. (1988). Growth and physical performance relative to the timing of the adolescent spurt. *Exercise and Sport Sciences Reviews, 16,* 503-540.

Bevis, C., & Nutter, J. B. (1977, November). *Changing street layouts to reduce residential burglary.* Paper presented at annual meeting of the American Society of Criminology, Atlanta, Georgia.

Bjor, J., Knutsson, J., & Kuhlhorn, E. (1992, July). The celebration of midsummer eve in Sweden—A study in the art of preventing collective disorder. *Security Journal, 3,* 169-174.

Bollens, J. C., & Schmandt, H. J. (1970). *The metropolis, its people, politics, and economic life.* New York: Harper & Row.

Booth, C. (1902). *Life and labour of the people in London.* London: Macmillan.

Bowden, M. J. (1975). Growth of the central business districts in large cities. Chapter 2 in L. F. Schnore (Ed), *The new urban history.* Princeton, NJ: Princeton University Press.

Brantingham, P. J., & Brantingham, P. L. (1989). *Patterns in crime.* New York: Macmillan.

Brantingham, P. J., and Brantingham, P. L. (Eds.). (1990). *Environmental criminology.* Prospect Heights, IL: Waveland.

Brantingham, P. L. (1979). Planning, development designs and crime. In S. Warner & L. Hill (Eds.), *Designing out crime: Crime prevention through environmental design (CPTED).* Conference sponsored by the Australian Institute of Criminology and NRMA Insurance.

Brantingham, P. L., & Brantingham, P. J. (1984). Mobility, notoriety and crime: A study in crime patterns of urban nodal points. *Journal of Environmental Systems, 11,* 89-99.

Braudel, F. (1979). *The structures of everyday life: The limits of the possible.* New York: Harper & Row.

Briar, S., & Piliavin, I. (1965). Delinquency, situational inducements and commitment to conformity. *Social Problems, 13,* 35-45.

California Office of the Attorney General. (1989). *Homicide in California.* Sacramento: Department of Justice, Bureau of Criminal Statistics and Special Services.

Carron, A. V., & Bailey, D. A. (1974). Strength development in boys from 10 through 16 years. *Monographs of the Society for Research in Child Development, 39* (Serial No. 157).

Clarke, R. V. (1978). *Tackling vandalism.* London: HMSO.

Clarke, R. V. (1983). Situational crime prevention: Its theoretical basis and practical scope. In M. Tonry & N. Morris (Eds.), *Crime and justice: An annual review of research* (Vol. 4, pp. 225-256). Chicago: University of Chicago Press.

Clarke, R. V. (Ed.). (1992). *Situational crime prevention: Successful case studies.* New York: Harrow & Heston.

Clarke, R. V., & Felson, M. (Eds.). (1993). *Routine activity and rational choice: Advances in criminological theory* (Vol. 5). New Brunswick, NJ: Transaction Books.

Clarke, R. V., & Harris, P. M. (1992). Auto theft and its prevention. In M. Tonry (Ed.), *Crime and justice: A review of research* (Vol. 16, pp. 1-54). Chicago: University of Chicago Press.

Clarke, R. V., & Lester, D. (1989). *Suicide: Closing the exits.* New York: Springer-Verlag.

Clarke, R. V., & Mayhew, P. (1988). The British gas suicide story and its criminological implications. In M. Tonry & N. Morris (Eds.), *Crime and justice* (Vol. 10, pp. 79-116). Chicago: University of Chicago Press.

Cloward, R. A., & Ohlin, L. E. (1960). *Delinquency and opportunity: A theory of delinquent gangs.* New York: Free Press.

Cohen, A. K. (1955). *Delinquent boys: The culture of the gang.* New York: Free Press.

Cohen, L. E., & Felson, M. (1979). Social change and crime rate trends: A routine activity approach. *American Sociological Review, 44,* 588-608.

Coleman, A. (1985). *Utopia on trial: Vision and reality in planned housing.* London: Hilary Shipman.

Coleman, J. C. (1980). *The nature of adolescence.* New York: Methuen.

Colquhoun, P. (1969). *A treatise on the police of the metropolis.* (Originally printed in London, 1795.) Montclair, NJ: Patterson-Smith.

Consumer Reports. (1980). *I'll buy that: Fifty small wonders and big deals that revolutionized the lives of consumers.* Mt. Vernon, NY: Consumers Union.

Cornish, D., & Clarke, R. V. (Eds.). (1986). *The reasoning criminal.* New York: Springer-Verlag.

Cromwell, P. F., Olson, J. N., & Avary, D. W. (1991). *Breaking and entering: An ethnographic analysis of burglary.* Newbury Park, CA: Sage.

Crowe, T. D. (1990, Fall). Designing safer schools. *School Safety, 9,* 9-13.

Crowe, T. D. (1991). *Crime prevention through environmental design: Applications of architectural design and space management concepts.* Boston: Butterworth-Heinemann.

Cusson, M. (1983). *Why Delinquency?* Toronto: University of Toronto Press.

Cusson, M. (1993). A strategic analysis of crime: Criminal tactics as responses to precriminal situations. In R. V. Clarke & M. Felson (Eds.), *Routine activity and rational choice: Advances in criminological theory* (Vol. 5). New Brunswick, NJ: Transaction Books.

Decker, J. F. (1992). Curbside deterrence? Chapter 1 in R. V. Clarke (Ed.), *Situational crime prevention: Successful case studies.* New York: Harrow & Heston.

Deutsch, K. W. (1951). On social communication and the metropolis. In L. Rodwin (Ed.), *The future metropolis* (pp. 129-143). New York: George Braziller.

Dolmen, L. (Ed.). (1990). *Crime trends in Sweden, 1988.* Stockholm: National Council for Crime Prevention.

Downs, A. (1989, August). *The need for a new vision for the development of large U.S. metropolitan areas.* New York: Salomon Brothers.

Doyle, A. C. (1984). *The works of Sir Arthur Conan Doyle.* New York: Crown.

Duffala, D. C. (1976). Convenience stores, armed robbery and physical environmental features. *American Behavioral Scientist, 20,* 227-246.

Duncan, O. D. (1959). Human ecology and population studies. In P. M. Hauser & O. D. Duncan (1959), *The study of population: An inventory and appraisal* (pp. 678-716). Chicago: University of Chicago Press.

Easteal, P. W., & Wilson, P. R. (1991). *Preventing crime on transport: Rail, buses, taxis, planes.* Monsey, NY: Criminal Justice Press.

Eck, J. E., & Spelman, W. (1987). *Problem solving: Problem-oriented policing in Newport News.* Washington, DC: Police Executive Research Forum.

Ekblom, P. (1992). Preventing post office robberies in London: Effects and side effects. Chapter 3 in R. V. Clarke (Ed.), *Situational crime prevention: Successful case studies.* New York: Harrow & Heston.

Erickson, M., & Jensen, G. F. (1977). "Delinquency is still group behavior!": Toward revitalizing the group premise in the sociology of deviance. *Journal of Criminal Law and Criminology, 68,* 262-273.

Fattah, E. A. (1991). *Understanding criminal victimization: An introduction to theoretical victimology.* Ontario, Canada: Prentice-Hall.

Federal Bureau of Investigation, Department of Justice. (Annual). *Uniform Crime Reports: Crime in the United States.* Washington, DC: Government Printing Office.

Felson, M. (1983). Ecology of crime. In S. H. Kadish (Ed.), *Encyclopedia of crime and justice.* New York: Macmillan.

Felson, M. (1986). Routine activities, social controls, rational decisions and criminal outcomes. In D. Cornish & R. V. Clarke (Eds.), *The reasoning criminal* (pp. 119-128). New York: Springer Verlag.

Felson, M. (1987a). Routine activities and crime prevention in the developing metropolis. *Criminology, 25,* 911-931.

Felson, M. (1987b). *Products which go kaput when stolen.* Paper presented at annual meeting of the American Society of Criminology, November, Montreal, Canada.

Felson, M., & Cohen, L. E. (1981). Modeling crime rate trends—A criminal opportunity perspective. *Journal of Research in Crime and Delinquency, 18,* 138-164 (as corrected, 1982, *19,* 1).

Felson, M., & Gottfredson, M. (1984, August). Adolescent activities near peers and parents. *Journal of Marriage and the Family, 46,* 709-714.

Felson, R. B., & Steadman, H. J. (1983). Situational factors in disputes leading to criminal violence. *Criminology, 21*(1), 59-74.

Felson, R. B. (1993). Predatory and dispute-related violence: A social-interactionist approach. In R. V. Clarke & M. Felson (Eds.), *Routine activity and rational choice: Advances in criminological theory* (Vol. 5). New Brunswick, NJ: Transaction Books.

Ferri, E. (1897). *Criminal sociology.* New York: D. Appleton.

Fishman, R. (1987). *Bourgeois utopias: The rise and fall of the suburb.* New York: Basic Books.

Flanigan, J. (1993, February 15). Southeast shows how to nail jobs. *Los Angeles Times,* p. 1.

Gabor, T., Baril, M., Cusson, M., Elie, D., LeBlanc, M., & Normandeau, A. (1987). *Armed robbery: Cops, robbers and victims.* Springfield, IL: Charles C Thomas.

Gans, H. (1962). *The urban villagers.* New York: Free Press.

Garbarino, J. (1978). The human ecology of school crime: A case for small schools. In E. Wenk & N. Harlow (Eds.), *School crime and disruption: Prevention models.* Washington, DC: National Institute of Education.

Geason, S., & Wilson, P. R. (1990). *Preventing car theft and crime in car parks.* Monsey, NY: Criminal Justice Press.

Geason, S., & Wilson, P. R. (1992). *Preventing retail crime.* Monsey, NY: Criminal Justice Press.

Gibbs, J. (1975). *Crime, punishment and deterrence.* New York: Elsevier.

Gilfillan, S. C. (1935). *The sociology of invention.* (Reprinted 1970). Cambridge: MIT Press.

Gilmore, H. W. (1953). *Transportation and the growth of cities.* New York: Free Press.

Glaser, D. (1971). *Social deviance.* Chicago: Markham.

Glazer, N., & Moynihan, D. P. (1970). *Beyond the melting pot.* Cambridge: MIT Press.

Glick, P. C. (1984, January). How American families are changing. *American Demographics, 6,* 20-24.

Goffman, E. (1963). *Behavior in public places.* New York: Free Press.

Goldstein, H. (1990). *Problem-oriented policing.* New York: McGraw-Hill.

Gottfredson, D. C. (1985). Youth employment, crime and schooling: A longitudinal study of a national sample. *Developmental Psychology, 21,* 419-432.

Gottfredson, G. D., & Gottfredson, D. C. (1985). *Victimization in schools.* New York: Plenum.

Gottfredson, M., & Hirschi, T. (1990). *A general theory of crime.* Stanford, CA: Stanford University Press.

Gottman, J. (1961). *Megalopolis: The urbanized northeastern seaboard of the United States.* New York: Twentieth Century Fund.

Grasmick, H. G., Tittle, C. R., Bursik, R. J., Jr., & Arneklev, B. J. (1993, February). Testing the core empirical implications of Gottfredson and Hirschi's general theory of crime. *Journal of Research in Crime and Delinquency, 30*(1), 5-29.

Greenberger, E., & Steinberg, L. (1986). *When teenagers work: The psychological and social costs of adolescent employment*. New York: Basic Books.

Hawley, A. H. (1950). *Human ecology: A theory of community structure*. New York: Ronald.

Hawley, A. H. (1956). *The changing shape of metropolitan America: Deconcentration since 1920*. New York: Free Press.

Hawley, A. H. (1971). *Urban society: An ecological approach*. New York: Ronald.

Hayes, R. (1992). *Retail security and loss prevention*. Boston: Butterworth-Heinemann.

Heer, D. M., & Herman, P. (1990). *A human mosaic: An atlas of ethnicity in Los Angeles County, 1980-1986*. Panorama City, CA: Western Economic Research.

Hindelang, M., Gottfredson, M., & Garafolo, J. (1978). *Victims of personal crime: An empirical foundation for a theory of personal victimization*. Cambridge, MA: Ballinger.

Hindelang, M., Hirschi, T., & Weis, J. (1981). *Measuring delinquency*. Beverly Hills, CA: Sage.

Hirschi, T. (1969). *Causes of delinquency*. Berkeley: University of California Press.

Hirschi, T. (1983). Crime and the family. In J. Q. Wilson (Ed.), *Crime and public policy*. San Francisco: ICS.

Hitchcock, A. (Ed.). (1959). *My favorites in suspense*. New York: Random House, 1959.

Hobsbawm, E. J. (1969). *Bandits*. New York: Delacorte.

Hoover, E. M., & Vernon, R. (1959). *Anatomy of a metropolis*. Cambridge, MA: Harvard University Press.

Hope, T. J. (1982). *Burglary in schools: The prospects for prevention*. Research and Planning Unit Paper 11. London: Home Office.

Hunter, R. D., & Jeffery, C. R. (1992). Preventing convenience store robbery through environmental design. Chapter 16 in R. V. Clarke (Ed.), *Situational crime prevention: Successful case studies*. New York: Harrow & Heston.

Illinois Law Enforcement Commission (1984 and annually). *Crime in Illinois*. Springfield: State of Illinois.

Jackson, K. T. (1985). *Crabgrass frontier: The suburbanization of the United States*. New York: Oxford University Press.

Jacobs, J. (1961). *Death and life of great American cities*. New York: Random House.

Jeffery, C. R. (1971). *Crime prevention through environmental design*. Beverly Hills, CA: Sage.

Johnston, L. D., O'Malley, P. M., & Bachman, J. G. (1992). *Smoking, drinking and illicit drug use among American secondary school students, college students, and young adults, 1975-1991*. U.S. Department of Health and Human Services, National Institute on Drug Abuse. Washington, DC: Government Printing Office.

Kandel, D. (1978). *Longitudinal research on drug use.* Washington, DC: Hemisphere.

Kappeler, V. E., Blumberg, M., & Potter, G. W. (1993). *The mythology of crime and criminal justice.* Prospect Heights, IL: Waveland.

Katz, L. R. (1987). *Ohio arrest, search and seizure* (3rd ed.). Cleveland, OH: Banks-Baldwin.

Keane, C., Maxim, P. S., & Teevan, J. J. (1993, February). Drinking, driving, self-control and gender. *Journal of Research in Crime and Delinquency, 30*(1), 30-46.

Kelling, G. L., Pate, T., Dieckman, D., & Brown, C. (1974). *The Kansas City preventive patrol experiment: A summary report.* Washington, DC: Police Foundation.

Kett, J. (1977). *Rites of passage: Adolescence in America, 1790 to the present.* New York: Basic Books.

Kitagawa, E. M., & Bogue, D. J. (1955). *Suburbanization of manufacturing activity within metropolitan areas.* Chicago: University of Chicago Population Research and Training Center.

Klein, M. W. (1971). *Street gangs and street workers.* Englewood Cliffs, NJ: Prentice-Hall.

Klein, M. W. (1984). Offense specialization and versatility among juveniles. *British Journal of Criminology, 24,* 185-194.

Klein, M. W., Maxson, C. L., & Cunningham, L. C. (1991). "Crack," street gangs, and violence. *Criminology, 29*(4), 623-650.

Kochen, M. (Ed.). (1989). *The small world (a volume commemorating Ithiel de Sola Pool, Stanley Milgram, and Theodore Newcomb.* Norwood, NJ: Ablex.

Kowinski, W. S. (1985). *The malling of America.* New York: William Morrow.

Larson, R. C. (1972). *Urban police patrol analysis.* 1972. Cambridge: MIT Press.

Lemert, E. M. (1972). *Human deviance, social problems and social control* (2nd ed.). Englewood Cliffs, NJ: Prentice-Hall.

LeVine, N., & Wachs, M. (1985). *Factors affecting the incidence of bus crime in Los Angeles.* Report prepared for U.S. Department of Transportation.

Ley, D. (1988). Social upgrading in six Canadian inner cities. *Canadian Geographer, 32*(1), 31-45.

Lofland, L. H. (1973). *A world of strangers: Order and action in urban public space.* New York: Basic Books.

Los Angeles Times. (1993, January 23). Judge disallows Gates blocking public streets, p. 1.

Lowman, J. (1986). Street prostitution in Vancouver: Some notes on the genesis of a social problem. *Canadian Journal of Criminology, 28,* 1-16.

Luckenbill, D. F. (1977). Criminal homicide as a situated transaction. *Social Problems, 25,* 176-186.

Malina, R. M. (1990). Physical growth and performance during the transitional years (9-16). Chapter 2 in R. Montemayor, G. R. Adams, & T. P. Gullotta

(Eds.), *From childhood to adolescence: A transitional period?* Newbury Park, CA: Sage.

Maxson, C. L., Gordon, M. A., & Klein, M. W. (1985). Differences between gang and nongang homicides. *Criminology, 23,* 209-222.

Mayhew, P., Clarke, R. V., & Eliot, D. (1989). Motorcycle theft, helmet legislation, and displacement. *Howard Journal of Criminal Justice, 28,* 1-8.

Mayhew, P., Clarke, R. V., & Hough, M. (1992). Steering column locks and car theft. Chapter 2 in R. V. Clarke (Ed.), *Situational crime prevention: Successful case studies.* New York: Harrow & Heston.

Mayhew, P., Clarke, R. V., Sturman, A., & Hough, J. M. (1976). *Crime as opportunity.* London: HMSO.

McKenzie, R. D. (1934). Industrial expansion and the interrelations of peoples. In E. B. Reuter (Ed.), *Race and culture contacts.* New York: McGraw-Hill.

McLuhan, M. (1962). *The Gutenberg galaxy: The making of typographic man.* Toronto: University of Toronto Press.

McLuhan, M., & Fiore, Q. (1968). *War and peace in the global village.* Toronto: University of Toronto Press.

McPartland, J. M., & McDill, E. L. (1976). *The unique role of schools in the causes of youthful crime.* Report No. 216. Baltimore: Johns Hopkins University Center for Social Organization of Schools.

McPartland, J. M., & McDill, E. L. (1977). *Violence in schools: Perspectives, programs and positions.* Lexington, MA: Lexington.

Medrich, E., Roizen, J., Rubin, V., & Buckley, S. (1982). *The serious business of growing up: A study of children's lives outside school.* Berkeley: University of California Press.

Merton, R. K. (1957). *Social theory and social structure.* New York: Free Press.

Messner, S. F., & Tardiff, K. (1986). Economic inequality and levels of homicide: An analysis of urban neighborhoods. *Criminology, 24,* 297-317.

Michelson, W. (1976). *Man and his urban environment: A sociological approach.* Reading, MA: Addison-Wesley.

Milgram, S. (1970, March). The experience of living in cities. *Science, 167,* 1461-1468.

Montemayor, R., Adams, G. R., & Gullotta, T. P. (Eds.). (1990). *From childhood to adolescence: A transitional period?* Newbury Park, CA: Sage.

Moore, M. H. (1992). Problem-solving and community policing. In M. Tonry & N. Morris (Eds.), *Crime and justice: A review of research* (Vol. 15, pp. 99-158). Chicago: University of Chicago Press.

Mumford, L. (1961). *The city in history.* New York: Harcourt Brace Jovanovich.

Nelson, H. J., & Clark, W. A. V. (1976). *Los Angeles: The metropolitan experience.* Cambridge, MA: Ballinger.

Newman, O. (1972). *Defensible space: Crime prevention through urban design.* New York: Macmillan.

Newman, O. (1980). *Community of interest*. Garden City, NY: Anchor.

Norman, D. A. (1988). *The psychology of everyday things*. New York. Basic Books.

Ogburn, W. F. (1964). *On culture and social change: Selected papers*. Edited by O. D. Duncan. Chicago: University of Chicago Press.

Ogburn, W. F., & Nimkoff, M. F. (1955). *Technology and the changing family*. Boston: Houghton Mifflin.

Olweus, D. (1978). *Aggression in the schools: Bullies and whipping boys*. New York: Halsted.

Ostransky, L. (1978). *Jazz city: The impact of our cities on the development of jazz*. Englewood Cliffs, NJ: Prentice-Hall.

Panati, C. (1987). *Panati's extraordinary origins of everyday things*. New York: Harper & Row.

Park, R. E. (1967). *On social control and collective behavior: Selected papers*. Edited by R. H. Turner. Chicago: University of Chicago Press.

Pease, K. (1992). Preventing burglary on a British public housing estate. Chapter 19 in R. V. Clarke (Ed.), *Situational crime prevention: Successful case studies*. New York: Harrow & Heston.

Petroski, H. (1992). *The pencil: A history of design and circumstance*. New York: Knopf.

Petroski, H. (1993). *The evolution of useful things: How everyday artifacts— from forks and pins to paper clips and zippers—came to be as they are*. New York: Knopf.

Pool, I. de S. (Ed.). (1977). *The social impact of the telephone*. Cambridge: MIT Press.

Poyner, B. (1983). *Design against crime: Beyond defensible space*. London: Butterworth.

Poyner, B. (forthcoming). What works in crime prevention: An overview of evaluations. *Crime Prevention Studies, 1*.

Poyner, B., & Webb, B. (1991). *Crime free housing*. Oxford, UK: Butterworth.

Rannals, J. (1955). *The core of the city*. New York: Columbia University Press.

Rapoport, A. (1977). *Human aspects of urban form: Towards a man-environment approach to urban form and design*. Elmsford, NY: Pergamon.

Reiss, A. J., Jr. (1988). Co-offending and criminal careers. In M. Tonry & N. Morris (Eds.), *Crime and justice: An annual review of research* (Vol. 10, pp. 117-170). Chicago: University of Chicago Press.

Reuter, P. (1984). *Disorganized crime: Illegal markets and the Mafia*. Cambridge: MIT Press.

Richards, L. G., & Hoel, L. A. (1980). "Planning procedures for improving transit station security." *Transportation Quarterly, 34*(3), 335-375.

Ricklefs, R. E. (1979). *Ecology*. New York: Chiron.

Roncek, D. W., & Lobosco, A. (1983). The effect of high schools on crime in their neighborhoods. *Social Science Quarterly, 64*, 598-613.

Roncek, D. W., & Maier, P. A. (1991, November). Bars, blocks and crimes revisited: Linking the theory of routine activities to the empiricism of "hot spots." *Criminology, 29*(4), 725-754.

Ruggiero, M., Greenberger, E., & Steinberg, L. (1982). Occupational deviance among first-time workers. *Youth and Society, 13,* 423-448.

Salisbury, G. T. (1984). *Street life in medieval England.* Oxford: Oxford University Press.

Sampson, R. J. (1987). Urban black violence: The effect of male joblessness and family disruption. *American Journal of Sociology, 93,* 348-382.

Schoff, H. K. (1915). *The wayward child.* Indianapolis: Bobbs-Merrill.

Schumacher, E. F. (1973). *Small is beautiful: Economics as if people mattered.* New York: Harper & Row.

Seward, R. R. (1978). *The American family: A demographic history.* Beverly Hills, CA: Sage.

Shaw, C., & McKay, H. (1931). *Social factors in juvenile delinquency.* Washington, DC: Government Printing Office.

Shaw, C., & McKay, H. (1942). *Juvenile delinquency and urban areas.* Chicago: University of Chicago Press.

Shearing, C. D., & Stenning, P. C. (1992). From the Panoptican to Disney World: The development of discipline. Chapter 22 in R. V. Clarke (Ed.), *Situational crime prevention: Successful case studies.* New York: Harrow & Heston.

Sherman, L. (1983). Patrol strategies for police. In J. Q. Wilson (Ed.), *Crime and public policy.* San Francisco: ICS.

Sherman, L., Gartin, P. R., & Buerger, M. E. (1989). Hot spots of predatory crime: Routine activities and the criminology of place. *Criminology, 27,* 27-56.

Simmel, G. (1969). Metropolis and mental life. In R. Sennett (Ed.), *Classic essays on the culture of cities.* New York: Appleton-Century-Crofts.

Simmons, R., & Blyth, D. (1987). *Moving into adolescence: The impact of pubertal change and school context.* New York: Aldine.

Sloan-Howitt, M., & Kelling, G. D. (1992). Subway graffiti in New York City: "Gettin' up" vs. "meanin' it and cleanin' it." Chapter 21 in R. V. Clarke (Ed.), *Situational crime prevention: Successful case studies.* New York: Harrow & Heston.

Smith, L. (1971). Space for the CBD's function. In L. S. Bourne (Ed.), *Internal structure of the city: Readings on space and environment* (pp. 352-360). New York: Oxford University Press.

Smith, S. J. (1986). *Crime, space and society.* Cambridge, UK: Cambridge University Press.

Sommer, R. (1969). *Personal space.* Englewood Cliffs, NJ: Prentice-Hall.

Southall, D., & Ekblom, P. (1985). *Designing for car security: Towards a crime-free car* (Crime Prevention Unit Paper No. 4). London: HMSO.

Stahura, J. M., & Huff, R. C. (1986). Crime in suburbia, 1960-1980. In R. M. Figlio, S. Hakim, & G. F. Rengert (Eds.), *Metropolitan crime patterns* (pp. 55-70). Monsey, NY: Willow Tree.

Storstockholms Lokaltrafic [Greater Stockholm Metro]. (no date). The world's longest art gallery—The Stockholm metro, Stockholm.

Sutherland, E. H. (1956). *The professional thief.* Chicago: University of Chicago Press.

Sutherland, E. H., & Cressey, D. R. (1974). *Criminology* (9th ed.). Philadelphia: J. B. Lippincott.

Sweet, J. A., & Bumpass, L. L. (1987). *American families and households.* New York: Russell Sage.

Tanner, J. M. (1962). *Growth at adolescence.* Oxford, UK: Blackwell Scientific.

Thornberry, T., & Chriatiansen, R. L. (1984). Unemployment and criminal involvement: An investigation of reciprocal causal structures. *American Sociological Review, 49,* 398-411.

Toby, J. (1983). Crime in the schools. In M. Tonry & N. Morris (Eds.), *Crime and justice, an annual review of research* (Vol. 4, 225-256). Chicago: University of Chicago Press.

Toch, H., & Grant, J. D. (1991). *Police as problem solvers.* New York: Plenum.

Tonry, M., & Morris, N. (Eds.). (1990). *Drugs and crime: Vol. 13. Crime and justice.* Chicago: University of Chicago Press.

Tremblay, P. (1993). Searching for suitable co-offenders. In R. V. Clarke & M. Felson (Eds.), *Routine activity and rational choice: Advances in criminological theory* (Vol. 5). New Brunswick, NJ: Transaction Books.

U.S. Bureau of Alcohol, Tobacco, and Firearms (various years). *Annual Report.* Washington, DC: Government Printing Office.

U.S. Bureau of the Census. (1950). *U.S. census of population.* Washington, DC: Government Printing Office.

U.S. Bureau of the Census. (1960). *U.S. census of population.* Washington, DC: Government Printing Office.

U.S. Bureau of the Census. (1970). *U.S. census of population.* Washington, DC: Government Printing Office.

U.S. Bureau of the Census. (1973). *Who's home when* (Working Paper No. 37). Washington, DC: Government Printing Office.

U.S. Bureau of the Census. (1974). *County business patterns.* Report CBP-74-1. Washington, DC: Government Printing Office.

U.S. Bureau of the Census. (1980a). *U.S. census of population* [Vol. 1, Chapter A (PC80-1-A)]. Washington, DC: Government Printing Office.

U.S. Bureau of the Census. (1980b). *U.S. census of population: Metropolitan statistical areas* [Supplementary report (PC80-S1-18)]. Washington, DC: Government Printing Office.

U.S. Bureau of the Census. (1986). *County business patterns.* Report CBP-86-1. Washington, DC: Government Printing Office.

U.S. Bureau of the Census (various years). *Statistical abstract of the United States.* Washington, DC: Government Printing Office.

U.S. Department of Education. (1978). *Safe school study.* Washington, DC: Government Printing Office.

U.S. Department of Education. (annual). *Digest of education statistics.* Washington, DC: Government Printing Office.

U.S. Department of Education. (annual). *Statistics of public elementary and secondary school systems.* Washington, DC: Government Printing Office.

U.S. Department of Justice. (1988). *Special report: International crime rates.* Bureau of Justice Statistics. Washington, DC: Government Printing Office.

U.S. Department of Justice. (annual). *Sourcebook of criminal justice statistics.* Washington, DC: Government Printing Office.

U.S. Department of Justice. (various years). *Criminal Victimization in the United States.* Washington, DC: Government Printing Office.

U.S. Department of Labor. (1991). *Dictionary of occupational titles* (4th ed.). Indianapolis, IN: Jist Works.

U.S. Department of Transportation. (1992, December). Edge city and ISTEA— Examining the transportation implications of suburban development patterns. *Searching for solutions: A policy discussion series* (No. 7). Federal Highway Administration. Washington, DC: Government Printing Office.

Van Dijk, J., & Junger-Tas, J. (1988). Trends in crime prevention in the Netherlands. In T. Hope & M. Shaw (Eds.), *Communities and crime reduction.* London: Her Majesty's Stationery Office.

von Hirsch, A. (1976). *Doing justice: The choice of punishments.* New York: Hill & Wang.

Walker, S. (1989). *Sense and nonsense about crime: A policy guide* (2nd ed.). Belmont, CA: Brooks-Cole.

Whyte, W. F. (1961). *Street corner society.* New York: Free Press.

Whyte, W. H. (1988). *City: Rediscovering the center.* New York: Doubleday.

Wigginton, E. (1972). *The Foxfire Book.* Garden City, NY: Doubleday.

Wigginton, E. (1973). *Foxfire 2.* Garden City, NY: Doubleday.

Wigginton, E. (1975). *Foxfire 3.* Garden City, NY: Doubleday.

Wigginton, E. (1977). *Foxfire 4.* Garden City, NY: Doubleday.

Wigginton, E. (1979). *Foxfire 5.* Garden City, NY: Doubleday.

Wigginton, E. (1980). *Foxfire 6.* Garden City, NY: Doubleday.

Wikstrom, P.-O. (1985). *Everyday violence in contemporary Sweden: Situational and ecological aspects* (Report No. 15). Stockholm: National Council for Crime Prevention.

Wirth, L. (1964). *On cities and social life: Selected papers.* Edited by A. J. Reiss, Jr. Chicago: University of Chicago Press.

World Almanac and Book of Facts. (1991). New York: Pharos.

Wrong, D. H. (1961). The oversocialized conception of man in modern sociology. *American Sociological Review, 26,* 183-193.

Wycoff, M. A. (1982). *Role of the municipal police: Research as a prelude to changing it.* Washington, DC: Police Foundation.

Author Index

Subject Index